A gift for

_____

from

_____

The AUNTS' Book

FOR THE AUNT WHO'S

Best AT Everything

CAROLINE HUGHES

Michael O'Mara Books Limited

First published in Great Britain in 2010 by
Michael O'Mara Books Limited
9 Lion Yard
Tremadoc Road
London SW4 7NQ

A CIP catalogue record for this book is available from the British
Library.

Papers used by Michael O'Mara Books Limited are natural,
recyclable products made from wood grown in sustainable forests.
The manufacturing processes conform to the environmental
regulations of the country of origin.

ISBN: 978-1-84317-459-2

1 2 3 4 5 6 7 8 9 10

www.mombooks.com

Cover design by Angie Allison from an original design by
Blacksheep Design.

Designed and typeset by K.DESIGN, Winscombe, Somerset
Illustrations by Robyn Neild
Printed and bound in England by Clays Ltd, St Ives plc

For Jack and Daisy

Contents

CONTENTS

Introduction: Why it's Great to be an Aunt

There's no one in the world like an aunt. With all the wisdom and kindness of a parent, but without the lectures on tidy rooms or being responsible, an aunt gets to enjoy a very special bond with her nephews and nieces. With them, she can relive the silliest bits of her youth, really let her hair down and feel five, ten or fifteen again.

> 'Only an aunt can give hugs like a mother,
> keep secrets like a sister, and share love like a friend.'
> SPANISH PROVERB

- Being an aunt means you've got a front-row seat for the special occasions in a child's life – first steps, first day of school, first dance on their wedding day. Luckily for us aunts, though, we can head home when tantrums or arguments flare up and the serious parenting needs to be done.

- An aunt can take up a vital neutral position in the middle of family dramas, even when the niece or nephew in question is in the wrong. As an aunt, you can offer your advice, support and a friendly wink when the going gets tough.

- An aunt will let easy goals go through her legs and past her feet when football skills are being practised.

- Aunts will listen to teenage confessions about bad break-ups, first experiences with alcohol and failed exams without having to ground anyone.

- Aunts can pass on lots of embarrassing stories about parents when they were young, taking them down a notch or two.

AUNTS' WEBSITE

There's now a website created for and by aunts, to share stories, information and pearls of wisdom about being a wonderful auntie. So if you're a cyber-clever sort, check out www.savvyauntie.com and perhaps log on to share your own hints and tips for legions of aunts all over the world.

Preparing for Auntie-hood

No matter what age you are when you first become an aunt you're bound to feel like you're back at school all over again, but this time struggling to learn the ABCs of being a proper grown-up. All of a sudden you're responsible for buying Christmas presents, not tearing off the red and gold paper under the tree yourself. Conversations at family Sunday lunches will switch from your latest career move or relationship crisis to how many minutes little Christopher slept last night and whether or not he likes puréed turnip. There are lots of learning curves when you become an aunt, but it's an upward sweep to a truly rewarding relationship.

When a new baby enters your family circle, it's natural that things will change. You may encounter some tricky – and some slightly disgusting – moments in the first months of your niece or nephew's life, but here's a quick guide to a few of the more baffling elements of the baby world, the Auntie ABCs:

A IS FOR ACCEPTANCE

One of the hardest bits about becoming an aunt is that there's no escaping you and your siblings are now fully fledged adults. You're no longer a part of the young, irresponsible generation

– soon a little person will be looking up to you as part of the family establishment. This is always a depressing thought, even if you are only young at heart, but try to remember that some women won't be as lucky to become an aunt at all. Give your best beaming auntie smile to any niece or nephew who seems to think that being over thirty means you already have one foot in the grave. To them, a week feels like a whole year, after all.

It can also be hard to acknowledge that your sibling – who you're used to seeing clutching an empty beer bottle rather than cradling an infant – has now formed their own family circle, when once you were members of the same little team. If this leaves you feeling a tinge of sadness, then all the more reason to throw yourself wholeheartedly into your auntie duties. You'll be an invaluable and much-loved addition to their new family unit with just a bit of thought and effort.

If you're tempted to rail against your new responsible status, don't forget that there are some childish perks to the job. Suddenly you're able to enjoy all the best, silly bits of being a kid again, combined with the freedom of being an adult: you can play the games, but also make the rules. This involves getting out lots of toys, watching cartoons and playing catch in the garden until the sun goes down. But combined with being able to have a nice glass of wine when you feel like it and to also nip off to read the papers when all the noise gets a bit too much.

Accepting with good grace that you're now the aunt, not the child, will lead to lots of fun in the future and will ensure that your relationship with your sibling stays as strong and happy as ever.

B IS FOR BABY-PROOFING

When a new baby joins the family it makes the normal domestic household turn into a battlefield of hazards. Things you wouldn't look at twice in an adult-only environment, like sockets and radiators, now need special attention. To help baby-proof your home, invest in a good basic parenting book that will point out the most common areas. Here are some basics to keep you busy in the meantime:

● Move all cleaning solutions, such as bleach and shoe polish, out of floor-level cupboards and onto the tallest shelf available.

● Invest in baby-gates for both the bottom and the top of stairs.

● Clear away any small items from tabletops and surfaces – like coins and paperclips – that could easily become a choking hazard to a curious baby.

● Make sure all medication is well out of a child's reach and stored in childproof containers.

● Put a fireguard round an open fire or hot radiator.

● If you have empty sockets at floor level, then invest in some socket covers and plug them in around the house.

A little baby-proofing will make time spent with your very young nieces and nephews stress-free for you, the parents and the baby.

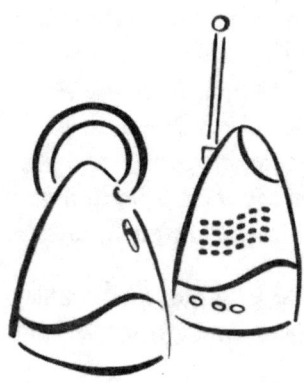

C IS FOR COPING

Being an aunt is a dirty job, but someone's got to do it. You'll naturally want to help your siblings as much as you can with their new brood and sooner or later that will mean a spot of babysitting. Long before you get to the stage of playing ball games in the park and baking cupcakes with your niece or nephew, there will be a good few months of *baby* babysitting. This is where new aunts can lose their nerve and plan a long holiday for, say, eighteen months. By the time they return, the new arrival will be bigger and easier to handle . . . maybe. But a bold and brave aunt will roll up her sleeves and brace herself. A red-faced wailing baby can make the steeliest nerve buckle, but with a few of these tips, you'll be able to cope with baby-sitting duty in no time:

- An upset baby can be soothed by keeping your voice low and calm while saying reassuring things, giving them a gentle pat on the back in the rhythm of a heartbeat and rocking them from side to side.

- Babies can pick up on panic in the people around them, so if you are feeling on edge take ten seconds to collect yourself in a quiet space. Try to avoid caffeine or alcohol as this could make you more jittery.

- Don't wear anything you're particularly attached to on your babysitting jaunt – you're likely to get stains from food, milk . . . and other things that you can well imagine.

- Ask your sibling for a full, frank list of instructions – don't be afraid to ask what might seem like stupid questions.

- Very young babies love to look at black and white in contrast, due to the development of their eyes in the first few months, so if you have a black-and-white striped T-shirt it may just give you the advantage.

GOING SHOPPING

If you'd like to buy a little something for the smallest member of your newly expanded family, it can seem overwhelming to step into a department store and see rails and rails of baby clothes in all sorts of shapes, sizes, materials and colours. Here are a few golden rules to follow before you flex the plastic:

- All-in-one romper suits with long sleeves are a good staple buy. Don't be too tempted to buy cute little shoes or hats for newborn babies: they may look adorable in the shop, but they probably won't be very practical.

- Check the label to see what the clothing is made of before you buy – pure organic cotton is best, but it might take a big bite out of your budget. Whatever you can afford, avoid polyester or other similar synthetic materials.

- Wait until the baby is born before buying clothes as often 'newborn' clothes are already too small.

- Pink for girls and blue for boys is just *so* last century. Don't forget there are a million colours out there and both nephews and nieces look gorgeous in green, yellow, red, purple, turquoise and orange. As well as being more original and fun, picking a more gender-neutral colour is a wise buy as it means items can be passed on to the next new baby, whether it's a he or a she.

AUNTS, KNOW YOUR LIMITS!

Having a new baby in the family is an exciting time for everyone and you might be dying to get stuck straight in to your auntie responsibilities. But don't rush round to your sibling's house the day they get home from the hospital. The new family will need lots of time to themselves to adjust to the new bundle of joy in their midst. Wait until you've been invited to visit and, when you are, take along some practical lifesavers to help them out while they're getting to grips with nappy changing and feed times: one or two meals you've cooked that they can stick in the freezer; some essentials like bread, milk and a newspaper; and maybe even a bottle of something sparkly to wet the baby's head in style! If you've had children yourself you'll know how grateful the new parents will be for any help offered, but they will have their own way of doing things so don't be offended if they're not up to visitors for a while.

As your niece or nephew grows older, you may be tempted to offer your thoughts and advice on how they should eat, sleep, play and be disciplined. This will obviously come from a wish to help, but it may sound to new parents like unhelpful criticism. Even if you've got many years of parenting under your own belt do try and remember that no one has a perfect rule book on parenting; it's something that changes with each set of parents in different situations. Always give your thoughts if you're asked, and be ready to help if things go a tad awry, but remember that no one likes a backseat auntie.

'Visit your aunt, but not every day; and call
at your brother's, but not every night.'
BENJAMIN FRANKLIN,
AMERICAN PRESIDENT AND INVENTOR (1706–1790)

Which Aunt Are You?

Every aunt has a special talent or gift that makes them extra special. Would your nieces and nephews say you were Girly, Cosy or Outdoorsy? Do you challenge them to a second game of football or a second helping of custard? Look through these profiles and see if you can recognize your own auntie style.

STRICT AUNTIE

There's no sneaking a hand into the biscuit jar when this aunt's around. She's a stickler for the rules and watching your Ps and Qs. She may be a bit stern, but she really just wants to help mould her nephews and nieces into polite, kind young people.

MOST LIKELY TO SAY: 'No feet on the furniture.'
LEAST LIKELY TO SAY: 'Why not go and jump on my bed? It's really springy and I don't mind if you keep your shoes on.'

PROS: A strict aunt is usually hot on organization so her house is always nice and tidy and she'll never forget to send a card in time for birthdays.
CONS: Sometimes there's enough telling off at home, without being sent to the naughty step by a bossy aunt as well.

FAMOUS AUNTS

American singer and TV star Jessica Simpson decided she was going to be a spoily sort of aunt even before her nephew Bronx was born. She said: 'I'm going to spoil the kid rotten, that's for sure. I think my sister's going to be pretty strict, actually, because she's been so good throughout her pregnancy.' When Bronx arrived, Jessica showed her credentials as a devoted and adoring aunt by declaring: 'Bronx is beyond precious. I'm over the moon with joy.' It's not just the everyday aunts who are convinced the children in their family are the most wonderful in the world!

GIRLY AUNTIE

A real shopping queen, the Girly Auntie loves everything a real girly girl should: shoes, gossiping and getting her nails done. If you have to choose her birthday present you know there's one colour to go for: pink.

MOST LIKELY TO SAY: 'I love those gorgeous heels in the window!'

LEAST LIKELY TO SAY: 'I probably have enough shoes, I won't buy any more.'

PROS: The ideal person to have with you for hunting out the best sale bargains and shopping till you drop.

CONS: The mammoth shopping trips and spa weekends might not be so good for your bank balance.

TRENDY AUNTIE

The Trendy Auntie always has the latest in cool clothes, must-have gadgets and hip new music. She's up on all the celebrity gossip and the most popular TV shows before you've even heard a whisper about them.

MOST LIKELY TO SAY: 'Have you seen my latest iPhone app?'
LEAST LIKELY TO SAY: 'Have you seen my slippers?'

PROS: This aunt is bound to have all the newest albums to borrow.
CONS: She might be a little too old to pull off tight white jeans from Topshop.

COSY AUNTIE

She's happiest when snuggled up on the sofa, in front of a warming fire, maybe with a good DVD on or some knitting in her lap. The Cosy Auntie will cook up big, wholesome dinners like chicken pie and lasagne, and always offer you seconds.

MOST LIKELY TO SAY: 'More apple pie?'
LEAST LIKELY TO SAY: 'Shall we go out clubbing tonight?'

PROS: A Cosy Auntie will always have top quality, easy recipes to borrow for a short-notice dinner party.
CONS: All those comforting, heavy dinners may lead to a slightly tight waistband after a while.

OUTDOORSY AUNTIE

A fan of everything active and sporty, the Outdoorsy Auntie will be the first one to suggest a long walk after a big Christmas dinner. She's positively allergic to the sofa and much happier with her walking boots on.

MOST LIKELY TO SAY: 'Anyone for tennis?'
LEAST LIKELY TO SAY: 'Anyone for Scrabble?'

PROS: No team is ever short of a player for football in the park or Frisbee in the back garden.
CONS: Just when everyone else fancies a cup of coffee and a biscuit, she's getting her Rollerblades out . . .

PARTY AUNTIE

A wild child at heart, this aunt is a real live wire. The first on the dance floor at any family wedding, she'll also be the last to leave it. She's the one that really gets the party started.

MOST LIKELY TO SAY: 'Oh, I love this song. Turn it up!'
LEAST LIKELY TO SAY: 'I'll just sit here and watch you young things.'

PROS: There's never a dull moment with her around and family occasions feel more like festive carnivals.
CONS: Spending an evening with her can lead to sore feet – and a sore head – the next morning.

EDUCATING AUNTIE

She's always planning trips to interesting museums and galleries and showing everyone the photos from her latest weekend break to a city full of cultural sights. The Educating Auntie will be able to recommend a good book, foreign film or piece of classic music at the drop of a hat.

MOST LIKELY TO SAY: 'I just finished *War and Peace* – you should borrow it.'

LEAST LIKELY TO SAY: 'I just watched a marathon of *Friends* episodes today – and they were all repeats.'

PROS: Without a doubt, the best family member to have on your team when playing a quiz game.

CONS: It's hard to persuade this aunt to indulge in a chick flick at the local cinema when some serious slobbing-out time is needed.

The Babysitters' Club

HOW TO COPE WITH BABYSITTING DUTIES FOR THE FIRST TIME

The first solo babysitting experience can fray the nerves of even the most rock-steady aunt. Never fear, unsure aunties, here's a survival guide for getting through that first babysitting session and proving that you're the go-to aunt who can be relied on.

DO YOUR HOMEWORK

No, this isn't what to lecture older nieces and nephews on after dinner, this is an order for you. If you've invested in a baby book and are looking after babies or toddlers, now is the time to consult it. It may give you some sanity-saving tips on how best to feed children, how to get them off to sleep easily and the basic signs of any illness to watch out for.

For older children, your homework should include getting the low-down on bedtimes, how much TV is allowed and which programmes they can watch and whether they really are allowed two bowls of ice cream. If you're going to be baby-sitting teenagers, make sure you ask the parents how long they are allowed to spend on the Internet or chatting on the phone to their friends, and whether friends are allowed to pop over.

If you are going to be looking after older kids or teenagers, it's also rewarding to think ahead and plan a few things to keep them busy. Pick up some magazines that are right for their age, dig out a board game or two and slot in a DVD if you're finding it really hard to keep them entertained. Kids that play up are usually kids that are bored, so keep them so busy that they don't have a spare brain cell to use plotting any kind of mischief (check out It's a Bake-Off, page 48 or Crafty Ideas, page 114).

For all your babysitting adventures, there are some basics that you should ask the parents before they disappear for a spell of much-deserved grown-up time:

● Where is the First Aid kit kept in the house?

● Do the children have any allergies? If so, how serious are they and what should you do if an allergy is aggravated?

● Emergency numbers: the parents' mobiles, the number of the place they're going to as a back-up and the out-of-hours number of their doctor. This is worst-case-scenario information, but it's good to be prepared.

THE 'A' TEAM

Just because you're a grown woman and a fabulous aunt, doesn't mean you're not entitled to go weak at the knees at the sound of a wailing baby, a five-year-old full of never-ending questions or the pounding music of a teen. If you want to give a helping sisterly hand, but the idea of babysitting leaves you trembling head to foot instead, why not team up with fellow aunts. You could suggest to other sisters or sisters-in-law that you tackle the babysitting shifts together to provide reassuring strength in numbers, or ask any friends that have aunt experience to join you. That way you have a fellow aunt there to back

you up when you say that Shark Attack programs are not allowed before bed. And when the kids are all safely tucked up with a glass of water and a story has been read, your A-Team can tuck their legs under them on the sofa with a small glass of something rewarding and share all the latest gossip. Perfect!

TEARS BEFORE BEDTIME

You might be holding it together during your babysitting baptism, but there could be a few other candidates for a wobbly lip: the kids. It's always scary for children to see Mum and Dad shut the door behind them and leave, seemingly forever, so don't be too disheartened if there are tears from your younger nieces and nephews. This is not a reflection on how they feel about you. Stay calm and reassuring at the sight of any emotional outbursts. Give the upset child a warm hug and, if it's almost bedtime, why not try saying this to give them a cheery way to look at things: 'The sooner you give a little smile, shut your eyes and go to sleep, the quicker morning will come when Mum and Dad will be home again.' If there's no other way to persuade them to feel happier, you can resort to the tried and tested method of a chocolate button . . .

BE A GOOD HOUSE GUEST

Yes, you will have worked hard into the small hours taking on babysitting labours, but that's no excuse for leaving a house strewn with toys, dirty dishes and puzzle pieces. Don't let your sibling's night out end in a grumble when they return home to

a mess; gather your strength with a cup of coffee, load the dishwasher, put the toys and books away and plump up the sofa cushions. Yes, you may feel absolutely beat after an evening of childcare, but just imagine how the parents feel doing it twenty-four hours a day. This is their one night off, so make it really last by leaving the house just as you found it (or even neater).

FAMOUS AUNTS

Ivanka Trump may not be the best aunt to call in times of babysitting crises. Ivanka, daughter of Donald and Ivana Trump and star of the US TV series of *The Apprentice*, admits she loves being an aunt and spoiling her nieces and nephews, but that the nitty-gritty jobs aren't quite her style: 'It's great being an aunt. Unless left alone with the child for extended periods of time, my responsibilities are quite easy. I can play until the baby ceases to be amused with me and then hand him back to his mom.'

The Breakfast Club

If you've had the kids to stay over and braved a whole night of babysitting then well done you. Your hardy nephews and nieces – and your good self – deserve a mighty breakfast to recuperate and it's only right to send them back to Mum and Dad full of energy and healthy stuff. Here are some very simple breakfast ideas to throw together for the kids. Just make sure to put an apron over your pyjamas.

AUNTIES' LITTLE SOLDIERS

Soft-boil some eggs and pop some bread into the toaster for a breakfast fit for an army. An egg needs four minutes in boiling water to be soft-boiled and eight minutes to be hard-boiled, if that's your preference. Politely demand a salute from your assembled troops before they sit down to tuck in.

PANCAKE TOWERS

Pancakes are a lovely treat for breakfast. Whip up some pancake batter (use a packet of ready-made batter if you're not a kitchen queen) and dollop a spoonful of the batter at a time

into a hot pan in which you've melted a knob of butter. Serve the pancakes with syrups, jams or some whipped cream. Sprinkle some berries over the top of your pancake stack to give a small nod to healthy eating. If you pile up enough pancakes, you'll create a tower of heavenly food – but it won't be long before it's demolished . . .

SUPER SMOOTHIES

A healthy way to start the day is with a tall, fruity drink. In a blender or food processor, pour in skimmed milk, ice cubes, and the peeled and chopped fruit of your choosing. This can be any of your favourite fruits, but those without too many seeds work best. You can buy bags of frozen summer fruits, which

are a great standby to have tucked away in the freezer. Blitz all the ingredients until you have a super smooth, vibrant breakfast to slurp down.

MODERN ART PORRIDGE

Oats are a great source of slow-release energy; perfect for kids who have lots of games to play and friends to see. You can make your porridge from scratch or use a ready-made packet. Once you have the porridge piping hot and in bowls, begin to splodge in teaspoons of yummy toppings: honey, raspberries, marmalade, seeds and nuts or chocolate drops. This will give you a splattered, delicious piece of modern art for those discerning palates among you.

A SWEET START

If you have a fussy eater in your care then slices of fruit in a handy pickupable size make a great, easy breakfast. Melon, pineapple, mango, apple and grapes are just some fruits that make a lovely, refreshing and vitamin-packed breakfast for growing bodies. Team them up with granola and yoghurt and you have a delicious, nutritious breakfast.

Party Time

Birthdays are the centre of your universe when you're a child and parties are the highlight of birthdays. Even though you're a mature auntie, you can probably think up at least three fantastic birthday memories right now. There's something very special about helping create a truly magical birthday for your nieces and nephews, and you get to have a whole heap of childish fun while you're at it. Here are some handy hints for an unforgettable party.

PARTY GAMES

Tried and tested family favourites

Musical statues
Everybody loves musical statues for the simple reason that it involves bopping around to lively music, ready to hold a silly pose the second the music stops. All you need is a stereo, space in the living room (push back the sofas and other furniture to make more room) and partygoers with lots of energy and some funky moves. Put a bit of a spin on this party classic by introducing new challenges. Ask the players to pull the funniest face they can when the music pauses and hold it as still as a statue. If there is even the smallest giggle then that player is out for this turn and must catch their breath on the sofa as they watch

all the other gurning statues battle on. Alternatively, you could ask the statues to stand on just one leg, absolutely still – a fraction of a wobble and it's game over.

Auntie says

Any old person can play 'Simon says', but only a trusty aunt can start a game of 'Auntie says'. Gather all your gang in front of you. Make sure they can all see you (stand on a stable chair if you're not the tallest of aunties). Everyone must follow your instructions when you begin them by saying 'Auntie says', but if they obey a direction that doesn't start that way, they are out. The trick to this game is to fool your players by keeping the instructions coming thick and fast: 'Auntie says . . . hop on one leg'; 'Auntie says . . . touch your toes'; 'Auntie says . . . squawk like a bird'; 'Put your right hand on your left elbow'. Anyone that followed that last task would have to take up a place on the sofa. Try to keep your players so busy thinking about what will come next that they rush to act before they remember they're supposed to wait for those magic words. Adjust your instructions to fit the age of the children at the party: nice and simple for the smaller children, with jumps, spins and waves, slightly harder for the older children and teens, with even a few dance moves or funny noises to make if you want to stir up some giggles. Hopefully they'll be laughing too much to listen properly.

Pass the parcel

If you have a spare hour or two before the party is due to kick off, then sit yourself down with a bag of individually wrapped sweets, some small party favours and a big roll of wrapping paper, or old newspapers if you're feeling ecological. Wrap the

best prize you have first. Keep it small, though, as anything too big will mean your parcel will become an unwieldy wrapping nightmare. A pack of playing cards, some marbles or a chocolate bar are ideal as final prizes. After you've wrapped this and are preparing to wrap it again, drop in a sweet. Keep going like this, wrapping lots of layers and putting in small sweets or

favours, leaving the occasional layer empty for that extra sense of jeopardy, until you're either out of presents, paper or the parcel will no longer fit through the door . . .

All the children should sit comfortably in a big circle on the carpet, close enough to be able to pass the parcel at high speed and really build the party buzz. Volunteer to operate the music – when it stops, the parcel belongs to the person who holds it.

The thermometer game

Before you go rooting around in the back of a drawer for a thermometer, don't panic. It's *you* that's the heat-measuring device in this game.

Pick a small object to hide – you can use anything that's to hand, from a Lego man to a small bouncy ball. Get the kids to wait outside the room and tuck the object away in a tricky, but not impossible hiding place.

After you've called the children in and they start to hunt out their prize, tell them if they're 'hot' or 'cold', in other words whether they're getting closer or further away from the object. You can tease them that they're so cold their fingers will freeze or that they're so hot they'll get sunburn. The sense of competition will get them giggling and racing round in no time.

Get creative

Tasty challenges

For this game you need: a pack of straws; some popcorn (but not the toffee-covered kind); four small bowls and a stopwatch. Put a small amount of popcorn in two of the bowls and pair

these bowls with an empty bowl each, with the paired bowls side-by-side. The object of the game is to pick up as many pieces of popcorn as you can and drop them into the empty bowl in two minutes. Sound easy? Well, it's not so simple when your hands are behind your back and you have to suck up each piece using a straw . . . The winner is the first to move all the popcorn across or to move the most in two minutes. Plus, the popcorn comes in very handy for a wind-down movie session later on in the day.

Pin the tail on the . . .
Most discerning kids might say that 'Pin the tail on the donkey' is a bit last century, so why not give it an up-to-date twist? All you need is a computer, a printer, a pair of scissors, some adhesive putty, a blindfold and a rough idea of what toys, films, TV shows or bands your nieces and nephews have an interest in at that moment. For example, if – like many aunts out there – you have a niece or nephew who knows all the songs from *High School Musical* back to front and inside out, search the Internet for a picture of one of its basketball-playing characters, preferably holding a basketball. Print two copies of this picture and from one of them carefully cut out the basketball shape. This will be your new 'tail'. When the full picture is tacked up on the wall, the blindfolded partygoer will have to try and match the basketball to where it is on the picture. Hey presto! 'Pin the tail on the donkey' becomes 'Pin the basketball on Troy'. You can also make a 'tail' from a pop star's microphone or guitar, a toy action hero's weapon or one half of a famous duo (for example, R2D2 to C3PO or Ken to Barbie). The best thing about this game is that it's quick to make, very economical and easy to update every year, plus the original fun

of the game still shines through when you've been blindfolded, spun around and have to take your best wild guess.

Games for older nieces and nephews

Have-a-go rock stars

It can sometimes be hard to find games to keep teenagers busy and interested at a party, especially when they get in the habit of saying everything is '*bor*-ing'. The one thing you can count on is that every teenager likes music of some sort or other (and plenty fancy themselves as pop stars in the making). Play to this strength by devising a 'Guess the intro' game. Before the party, do a little research into songs that are topping the charts that week and that are particularly catchy. Then also come up with a list of generation-defying crowd-pleasers that everyone knows (even if they won't admit it in public) and that have instantly recognizable intros. Good examples are 'Dancing Queen' by Abba, 'Bohemian Rhapsody' by Queen and 'Billie Jean' by Michael Jackson. At the party, divide your party people into two teams. Choose one particularly musically spirited member of each team to be the performer. They must perform the intro as best they can so the rest of their team can guess it quickly. They can make guitar, drum and synthesizer noises and even do a helpful mime or two, but absolutely mustn't sing any words. Air guitar is allowed, especially if it's bad. The winning team is the one that guesses the most songs on their turn. If the game goes down well, you can let the teens think of more intros on the spot until they really do become 'bored' and look for another pastime.

Truth or fiction?

This is an easy, laid-back game to play with teens who like to lounge and not use up too much energy, but who may have a very cheeky sense of humour. It's more of a conversation starter than a point-scoring competition, so ideal when you have a group of teenagers who aren't all friends already. In a circle, everyone has to take it in turns to say three things about themselves: two things should be true and one thing should be utterly made up. The trick is to think of two very interesting things no one might know about you and making up a lie that's interesting, but also believable. If the lie is too preposterous it will stand out like a sore thumb. If you've been to some far-out places on holiday or ever tried an extreme sport these will be ideal things to use as your truths. When you're thinking of a lie, try to think of a thing everyone could imagine you doing that's also quite adventurous, like accidentally bumping into a minor celebrity or swimming with dolphins.

The more you play, the craftier and more imaginative you'll become. Of course, a good aunt shouldn't encourage lying with her nieces and nephews, but a little embroidering of the truth for fun is another matter all together. If you really want to make it a brain-busting game, you can allow the players to interrogate each other, to gather handy background information and test the authenticity of their claims. Nieces and nephews who think on their feet will really excel at 'Truth or fiction?'.

PARTY PLANNER EXTRAORDINAIRE

If you have the time and the budget to help out in throwing the birthday party in question, why not suggest a theme? It's great fun for all the invited friends and family to come in costume, even if it's just a few silly accessories and it will set your niece or nephew's party apart from all the other run-of-the-mill pizza parties or swimming trips they might have been to. It also gives creative aunts a chance to flex their crafty muscles. Here are a few themes to start you thinking . . .

For sports nuts

Create a party invite that's laid out like the court of your youngest family member's favourite sport or make them from circles of coloured card to look like footballs or basketballs. As well as giving out the important information of the date, time

and venue of the party, the invite should ask everyone to come in their favourite sports teams' kit or dressed up like they were going to play their favourite outdoor activity. Trainers will be a must at this party.

If there's enough money in the kitty, take the birthday party group to a local leisure centre or sports hall and use the facilities there to have a go at trampolining, volleyball or short tennis with a qualified instructor on hand. If your budget is a bit more modest, then head to your local public park or a large garden with as many footballs, rugby balls, beach balls etc. as you can borrow from friends and family. Divide the partygoers into two teams and get the competitive juices flowing with mini games of well-known sports, or any that you care to make up yourself. Bring along prizes for first, second and runners-up places (no one should feel left out at a party, after all) and have a silly awards ceremony, finishing on a loud set of hip-hoorays for everyone who played.

For fairy-tale fans

You might well have a little nephew who likes to imagine slaying dragons or a young niece who loves any excuse to put on a princess dress, so why not have a fairy-tale themed party at home? The effort required is minimal, but the results can be magical. Buy some simple paper crowns from a fancy dress or party shop and get together lots of pens, glue, glitter and sequins for the partygoers to decorate their own crown when they arrive. While these are put aside and drying, sit everybody down for lunch. You can easily transform any table into something befitting a banqueting hall with a few simple tricks and

lots of imagination. Look out for brightly coloured disposable tablecloths, coloured plastic cups and silver-coloured plastic cutlery. Put together name cards with a gold pen on squares of black card, making sure you put a 'Sir' or 'Lady' in front of every name, as is fitting for such a royal household. Serve fruit punch as 'mead' and chicken legs as 'roast guineafowl'. If you're crafty enough to make your own 'Pin the tail on the . . .' game (see page 37), then you can really get the party in full swing with a homemade 'Pin the tail on the dragon'. When your knights and fair maidens begin to get a bit over-excited or partied-out, stick on their favourite Disney fairy story and enjoy some well-earned quiet time.

Culture Vulture

Aunts are there to be fun and kind, but they can also be surreptitious educators while no one is looking. If you're not happy to sit idly by while your nephews and nieces just watch TV and play computer games in their free time, why not expand their minds by suggesting you take them out for a spot of culture? You'll feel a wholesome glow in introducing your young relatives to some more enlightening entertainment. If you haven't indulged your cultural side for a while, here are some thought-starters.

SCIENCE MUSEUM

WHO WILL ENJOY IT: children from five to fifteen
AUNTIE EXHAUSTION RATING: lots of walking and talking, so
    8/10

A day trip to a hands-on interactive science museum will appeal to nieces and nephews of all ages, including those who love school and those who just like pressing buttons to see what happens. Many museums now have more than just models and diagrams – they have skeletons of weird and wonderful creatures, devices to blow giant bubbles and interactive displays

that play movie clips you can all watch together. As this isn't a school trip, let the kids skip the bits that don't interest them and try to answer as many of their questions as you can. If you're left lost for words when asked something like what electricity actually *is*, suggest that you all look it up together when you get home in an encyclopaedia or on the Internet. And don't forget to hit the gift shop on the way out, so your nieces and nephews have a nice little reminder of their fun day with their number one auntie.

FAMOUS AUNTS

Aunts can provide all sorts of inspiration for talented nieces and nephews. Gorgeous actress Rachel Weisz looked close to home when researching a role in which she played an astronomer; her 85-year-old aunt had been a scientist who dedicated her career to research. Rachel said: 'I had one real-life scientist in my world and that was my aunt.' Proof of how very useful and informative aunts can be.

MODERN ART GALLERY

WHO WILL ENJOY IT: children from five to seventeen
AUNTIE EXHAUSTION RATING: 5/10, as long as the strolling isn't too quick and there's a good coffee shop

Art is all about an individual's opinion on whatever painting or sculpture is in front of them: you can like it or loathe it, but you can't ever be wrong. Everybody's opinion is valid, and this includes the newest generation of your family. Start your nieces and nephews talking about what they're looking at by asking them which is their favourite, which they don't like and – most importantly – why the art makes them feel the way they do. Only keep the trip going for as long as you think the children's interest is sustained.

MUSICAL MATINEE

WHO WILL ENJOY IT: children from ten to seventeen
AUNTIE EXHAUSTION RATING: 6/10, with a definite sore throat
    factor after lots of singing

Give your nieces and nephews the chance to put on their best clothes and see a show by treating them to tickets to a matinee performance of a big all-singing, all-dancing musical. This doesn't necessarily mean a costly trip to a big city and top-price front-row tickets. Check out local universities and colleges in your area to see if there's a student production of a well-known musical happening, or ask around to see if there's an amateur dramatics group nearby. Either of these options will take the high stress and high cost out of a trip to the theatre, but you'll still have the same excuse to eat ice cream at the interval and sing along (if you know the words, that is).

Great musicals to watch with children include: *Grease*, *Chitty Chitty Bang Bang*, *The Wizard of Oz*, *Oliver!* and *Cats*. It's true that, in most cases, nieces will probably have more fun

picking out a glitzy outfit and doing their hair specially, but after twenty minutes of the show you can put your money on the nephews in the audience mouthing the words and nodding along to all the tunes too.

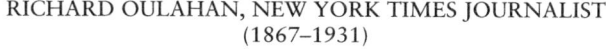

'The building has all the requisites of a great aunt. She is neither very pretty nor elegant, but she has enduring qualities of character.'

RICHARD OULAHAN, NEW YORK TIMES JOURNALIST (1867–1931)

It's a Bake-off

The simplest things are sometimes the most enjoyable and that's always true when you knock up some easy, hands-on treats with your nieces and nephews. These effortless recipes are perfect for when you need to entertain little ones on a rainy afternoon, and you can't go wrong with the holy trinity of fairy cakes, cookies and pizza.

FAIRY CAKES

Not only is whipping up cake mixture always wonderful fun, but when the cakes are cooled after cooking you can prolong the culinary entertainment by going to town on the decorations. Tubes of coloured icing are readily available, making it super simple to add patterns, shapes and words to the top of your cakes. Alternatively just stick to the good old-fashioned method of some icing sugar, a few drops of food dye and a little water. The bolder the better!

YOU WILL NEED:

12-hole bun tin and 12 paper cases
125 g (4½ oz) softened butter
125 g (4½ oz) caster sugar
2 medium eggs, lightly beaten
1 tsp vanilla extract
125 g (4½ oz) self-raising flour
2 tbsp milk

Makes 12

① Preheat the oven to 190°C/375°F/Gas mark 5. Put out your paper cases.

② Beat together the butter and sugar until the mixture is fluffy and a pale yellow colour. If you want a workout for your upper arms then use a wooden spoon and plenty of elbowgrease. If you want to take things easier, then don't feel too bad about plugging in the electric whisk.

③ Add the beaten egg to the bowl gradually, mixing as you go.

④ Add the vanilla extract and mix well.

⑤ With a sieve over the mixing bowl, sift in half the flour. Fold this flour into the mixture with your wooden spoon.

⑥ Add the milk and the rest of the flour and fold until all the ingredients are completely combined.

⑦ Fill your paper cases about two-thirds full, using one spoon to scoop up some mixture and another spoon to push the mixture into each case.

⑧ Put the tray into the preheated oven and bake for 12 minutes or until the cakes are risen and golden on top. If you're not sure whether the cakes are done, insert a skewer into the middle of one; if it comes out clean, the cakes are done, if there is some sticky cake mixture on it, pop them back in the oven for another few minutes.

⑨ Allow to cool for 10 minutes on a rack before removing from the tin.

Once you've mastered this classic staple of baking, you can get a bit adventurous and play with all sorts of tastes in your icing and toppings, especially if your niece or nephew has a particular favourite flavour.

Citrus icing with cherries

YOU WILL NEED:

100 g (3½ oz) icing sugar
2 tbsp freshly squeezed lemon or orange juice
12 glacé cherries, halved

Mix the juice into the icing sugar and stir until well blended. Using a teaspoon, drizzle the icing over the cakes when they are fully cooled. Top with the cherries, cut side down, while the icing is still soft.

Creamy chocolate icing

YOU WILL NEED:

150 g (5¼ oz) good quality dark chocolate, broken into chunks

150 ml (5¼ fl. oz) double cream

Melt the chocolate in a bowl over a pan of hot water. Pour in the cream and stir until blended. Then take the bowl off the pan – keep the children well back at this point – and leave the mixture to cool and thicken slightly. Spread the icing over the cakes with the back of a teaspoon.

COOL COOKIES

Cookies are a great snack to take with you on a long country walk or down to a beach picnic (if they last that long). Once you've got to grips with this recipe for chocolate chip, you can try adding dried fruit, nuts (so long as there are no allergies) and sweets – anything that takes your fancy (sorry, *their* fancy . . .).

YOU WILL NEED:

115 g (4¼ oz) butter

50 g (1¾ oz) caster sugar

110 g (4 oz) soft brown sugar

1 egg, beaten

1 tsp vanilla extract

170 g (6 oz) chocolate chips – milk, dark or white, or a mixture of all three, depending on your taste

155g (5½ oz) plain flour
½ tsp baking powder

Makes approx. 12 large cookies

① Preheat the oven to 190°C/375°F/Gas mark 5. Line a wide, flat baking tray with greaseproof paper.

② In a mixing bowl, beat the butter and both sugars together until light and fluffy, then stir in the beaten egg and vanilla extract.

③ Sprinkle in the chocolate chips of your choice (and any extras, like sweets) and mix well until they are evenly spread through the mixture.

④ In a separate bowl, mix together the flour and baking powder. Add a little of this at a time to your chocolate chip mixture until everything is combined and you have a soft dough.

⑤ Double-check everyone in the cooking party has washed their hands before this next step. Coat your hands in a little flour and then pick out a walnut-sized lump of dough from the bowl and roll it into a ball. If the mixture is too sticky and won't roll nicely, add another tablespoon of flour to the mix and try again.

⑥ Place each ball on the baking tray and press down lightly. Make sure you give each soon-to-be cookie plenty of space because they'll spread when you bake them.

⑦ Bake in the oven for 10–12 minutes. Take them out of the oven and leave them to cool for another 10 minutes, then move to a cooling rack.

⑧ Go to town with coloured icing and cake decorations for a more artistic tasty treat! This is especially fun if it's Easter, Halloween or Christmas – you can decorate them with a seasonal theme.

PIZZA TO GO, GO, GO!

If you're looking for a savoury snack to make with the kids then this recipe is ideal for hands-on and hungry children. This is more of an assembly line job than haute cuisine so it's ideal for young family members and kitchen-shy aunts.

To satisfy the fast-food urges of nieces and nephews, but give them a meal that will be nutritious as well, provide as many vegetable toppings as possible for these pizza breads. It's a great way to encourage kids to get to know what they're eating and try new foods too, as when the slicing is done and the knives put safely away they can have free rein to make whatever pizza they like. Prepare for some messy kitchen chaos . . .

YOU WILL NEED:
>   1 French stick loaf of bread
>   Olive oil
>   4 tomatoes
>   1 white onion
>   A handful of mushrooms
>   1 red bell pepper
>   A handful of fresh basil leaves
>   Salami slices
>   2 balls of mozzarella cheese

Salt and pepper
A pinch of dried
   oregano (optional)
A jar of ready-made
   pesto (optional)

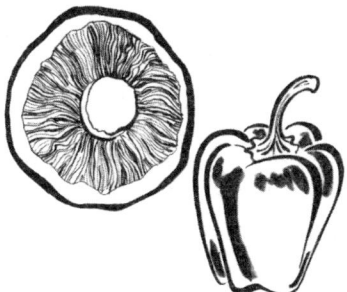

Serves 6

① Preheat the grill to a medium heat.

② Slice the French stick into short lengths. Cut down the middle of each length, as if you were about to make a sandwich. Lay each piece with the cut side facing up on a large baking tray.

③ Pour a little olive oil into a dish and let the kids brush the top of each slice of bread with oil using a pastry brush.

④ Slice up the tomatoes, onion, mushrooms and pepper as finely as you can – it's always best to keep sharp knives well away from little fingers, so make sure you do your slicing on a different kitchen surface from your nieces and nephews.

⑤ If you'd like to use some oregano or pesto on your pizza breads, sprinkle or spread on the bread at this stage.

⑥ Lay out the sliced vegetables for the kids to arrange on each bread slice. Then let them tear up the basil and scatter over the bread, and add salami slices if they want.

⑦ Let the kids tear the mozzarella balls into little pieces and dot them over the top of each slice.

⑧ Wearing an oven glove, slide the baking tray under the grill. Keep checking on the pizza breads and if the toppings look like they might be browning a little too much, turn down the heat. When the cheese has melted and the bread toasted, take them out, cool slightly and enjoy with some salad and a healthy glow of satisfaction.

SPECIAL AUNT STORIES

Ron Salisbury knew that his beloved aunt Dorothy's last wish was that she should be buried next to her husband. The one problem was that she hadn't been able to remember just where her late husband Frederick had been put to rest when he died forty-two years before. So Ron appealed to his local newspaper after Dorothy passed away and was over the moon when a funeral director got in touch with vital information. They had records showing his uncle's ashes had been scattered on a garden of remembrance nearby. Ron was able to reunite his aunt and uncle at long-last and was truly happy to have fulfilled Dorothy's final wish.

What Not to Say

If you're an auntie without children of her own, or an auntie whose children have long since grown up and flown the nest, playing your part in raising your nieces and nephews can seem like a bit of a family minefield. For starters, you want to help out as much as you can, but not tread on any parental toes; you want to give your nieces and nephews lots of lovely treats, but not turn them into spoilt brats; you want to be the favourite auntie, but you don't want to become a pushover, either. To help you pick a safe route through this puzzling territory, and to make sure you're being the best aunt to both your siblings and your nieces and nephews, here are some handy guidelines to avoid any tears before bedtime . . . for everyone involved.

PLAYING BY THE RULES

Your siblings may be laid-back parents or they may be ultra-strict. Regardless of how you were brought up and of what you feel is the best parenting style, as an aunt you should observe whatever method the parents have decided on. When or if you have your own children you can of course be the boss, but right now your role is to be a team player and a supportive cog in their family machine. Talk to your siblings about how they deal

with bad behaviour and if they're comfortable with you handing out any punishments should the situation arise.

Bite your tongue if you have to, or count to ten, but never undermine or neglect the decisions of the parents; after all, even though you're a treasured member of the family, it's the parents that bear the real brunt of responsibility here. Children respond well to consistency, so even if you're tempted to be the soft auntie and let them get away with the odd misdemeanour, you really won't be helping them in the long run.

DON'T SAY: 'Mum won't let you do that? Well, she's not here, so just this once . . .'

DO SAY: 'I'm not sure if Mum and Dad would allow that. Let's check with them, shall we?'

CLOWNING AROUND

It can be tempting to do anything and everything to become the number-one favourite aunt who gets all the hugs and attention from the kids, but do remember you're an adult, not a fellow child. By all means, indulge in a silly dance to the radio with them or kick through the autumn leaves in the park when you all have your walking boots on. But remember: even if you are – or just feel – young at heart, your nieces and nephews look up to you as a responsible adult. Monkey see, monkey do; so don't lead your monkeys astray. Focus on proper table manners, polite conversation with extra helpings of please and thank you, patient turn-taking and being noble in the face of defeat when you play games. No swearing. If any swear words do slip out, make sure you apologize to everyone and explain to your nieces

and nephews how you know it's a very bad word and you won't do it again.

DON'T SAY: 'Have I ever shown you how to throw peanuts and catch them in your mouth?'
DO SAY: 'I'd love some broccoli, thank you. Could you please pass the peas?'

SPILLING THE BEANS

Being a beloved aunt means you're privy to lots of personal information about your nieces' and nephews' lives, but do remember that you should always keep this to yourself. You know all the silly nicknames, the funny stories and the strange habits, but these home truths should most definitely stay *at home*. Little James won't appreciate you calling out his sickly sweet family nickname over the football pitch when you're cheering him on to score a goal and little Janet won't be laughing along when you tell her friends how she was always so scared of the dark when she has her classmates round for a sleepover. Think back to how everything seemed *so embarrassing* to you when you were growing up – especially all the old people in your family. Sadly, you now are one of the olds so try to break the cycle of blushes and keep the pet names and silly stories hidden away for when your nieces and nephews are grown-up enough not to care anymore.

DON'T SAY: 'Wasn't it sweet when Robert used to dress up in my pink skirt and pretend he was a ballerina?'
DO SAY: 'Yes, you were always very cool, even as a baby.'

FAMOUS AUNTS

Some aunts are always going to be biased about their gorgeous nieces and nephews, but some have more cause to be biased than others. Monica Weller is the aunt of the very gorgeous and famous actor Robert Pattinson, star of the *Twilight* movies. Monica said: 'He was always a good-looking boy and he does have a special something that makes people want to watch him. But at the same time, he is really just a very normal boy, with manners and charm, and I think girls find those qualities attractive.' I don't think anyone could argue with that . . .

ALL PLAY AND NO WORK . . .

Fun aunts are absolutely the right sort of aunts, but spoiling aunts take the fun one step too far. Yes, it may have been a drag that, when you were little, you were made to eat all your greens and mind your Ps and Qs, but if you hadn't what sort of person would you be now? Quite chubby and very rude, probably. And no aunt wants that for their young nieces and nephews. So, do try and remember that a few rules go a long way and teach your small family members how to respect others and take care of themselves. Keep naughty treats for really special occasions or to reward excellent behaviour. Don't be afraid of saying 'No' in moderation; you might get a stuck-out bottom lip in protest, but the love your nieces and nephews

have for you won't be diminished because they couldn't have three slices of chocolate cake for lunch.

DON'T SAY: 'Well, I suppose if you *really* want it . . .'
DO SAY: 'If you eat everything on your plate I might *think* about us having a scoop of ice cream each.'

Easter Bunny

If the emergence of spring puts a definite bounce in your step, then share your energy with your nieces and nephews with some fabulously fun seasonal activities. Perfect both for getting out and about on crisp, sunny spring days and for when you need to think of an indoor activity during those annoying April showers. And you can delight in making your nieces and nephews groan in embarrassment at all your terrible egg-related jokes. Let's get *cracking*!

EGG-CELLENT EGG DECORATING

It doesn't get more traditional than decorating real eggs at Easter and the mixture of creative expression and careful skill needed make it an absorbing bit of fun for everyone. Here's a step-by-step guide to some fabulous hand-decorated eggs:

● Take your eggs out of the fridge a few hours before you want to start the decorating process – it's much harder to work with them if they're cold. Hang on to the carton they came in, though, as this will come in useful a bit later.

- Use a large sewing needle – do this job yourself so that your nieces and nephews won't risk pricking themselves – and gently make a hole in each end of the egg.

- Push the needle all the way in through one of the holes. This will make sure the yolk will be broken inside.

- Use a kitchen skewer to enlarge one of the holes. Be careful that you don't crack the shell at this stage. You might literally end up with egg on your face.

- Hold the egg, with the enlarged hole facing downwards, over a small mixing bowl. Now for the fun bit the kids will love: gently blow through the small hole. All the white and broken yolk will now come out of the bigger hole and end up in the bowl below. (You'll have the ingredients for a nice omelette or plate of scrambled eggs for the young crafters later on.)

- When all the eggs you want to decorate are completely empty, carefully place them in a bowl of water so they're clean enough to start decorating. Lay some kitchen towel inside the egg carton and then stand the eggs – with the larger hole facing down – in their places to dry out and for any small bits of egg to seep out. Leave the eggs to dry like this for half an hour.

- When the eggs are completely dry, it's time to crack on with the decorating.

The kids are bound to have lots of creative ideas about what to draw, paint or stick on their eggs so assemble lots of different materials and let their imaginations run wild. Here's a list of everyday things that can make truly show-stopping eggs:

● Felt-tip pens for drawing on shapes, pictures or patterns.

● Thin paintbrushes for colouring in with poster paints, or adding details.

● Paints.

- Glitter and glitter glue for dazzling eggs.

- Small stickers in all sorts of shapes and colours. Seasonal stickers of chicks, lambs and flowers if you can find them.

- Feathers from craft shops or those picked up on a walk in the woods.

- PVA glue: not only will this stick on any fun embellishments, but if you apply a thin layer all over the egg once the design is complete it will give it a lovely glossy varnish. A little bit of PVA can also work wonders at patching up any tiny cracks in the eggs' shells.

- Food colourings. Seven or eight drops of a food colouring in a mug of warm water mixed with a tablespoon of white vinegar will form a perfect dip dye for your eggs. Plunge the egg into the cup as deeply as you want it covered – why not experiment with dipping the ends in different colours? Just make sure you let the dye dry between coats.

- Apply sequins and a ribbon as a finishing touch.

When the eggs are decorated with not an inch of plain shell in sight, assemble them in a basket on a bed of bright tissue paper and add flowers from the garden and a chocolate egg or two to make a glorious centrepiece for the family lunch table.

AN EGG-STRAORDINARY EASTER EGG HUNT

An Easter egg hunt is great fun, whether you have a garden and some good weather or just a living room and some imagination. If you want to avoid your nieces and nephews gorging themselves on too many chocolate eggs and you have some time in advance, cut out large egg-shapes in coloured card and cover these in sticky-backed plastic or take them to a local printing shop to be laminated. This will mean you can hide them in the garden outside without them going damp and soggy before they're found. Make two eggs larger than the others or put a gold star on a few of them. Hide the egg 'tokens' in flowerpots, under bushes and in the low branches of trees that the children could reach. Then, when the kids have run themselves out trying to find them, add up who has the most or who has the 'special' ones. The winner will get one chocolate egg as their prize and everyone else can have a small bag of mini chocolate eggs as a consolation prize. This way, a lot of exercise has been achieved with a minimal sugar rush to follow.

If you don't have access to a garden or it's raining, you can still hide the 'tokens' (or real chocolate eggs) in the living room under sofas, behind curtains and inside toy trucks. You might need to encourage the kids to take their search slowly as you're in a smaller space. If they can't find all the eggs, you can give them 'hotter' and 'colder' clues from the Thermometer game on page 36.

AN EASTER TREAT: CHOCOLATE NESTS
WITH CHOCOLATE EGGS

Everybody enjoys tucking in to one of these crunchy, chocolaty treats, just as much as they enjoy making them. It's a simple recipe that your nieces and nephews can help you with – as long as most of the mixture stays in the bowl and doesn't get sneaked into hungry little mouths! These will take just fifteen minutes to prepare, with thirty minutes or so of chilling time in the fridge afterwards.

YOU WILL NEED:

   100 g (3½ oz) butter at room temperature
   1 tbsp cocoa powder
   75 g (2½ oz) chocolate, broken into pieces
   75 g (2½ oz) golden syrup
   4 Shredded Wheat biscuits
   A bag of mini chocolate eggs to decorate
   12 paper cases

Makes 12

① On the hob, heat water in a pan until it's boiling (keeping nieces and nephews well away from the hob for this bit). Put a heatproof bowl on top of the pan so that it's heated by the steam rising from the boiling water.

② Put the butter, cocoa powder, chocolate and golden syrup into the bowl and stir gently until everything is melted and mixed together.

③ Carefully take the bowl off the pan (be careful of any steam escaping) and set it on a heatproof surface or chopping board. Then, call on your culinary assistants to crumble the Shredded Wheat biscuits into the bowl (this makes the 'twigs') and mix well.

④ Lay out the paper cases on a large plate or tray. Let the children put a generous dollop of the mixture into each case. Using the back of the spoon, press a well into the middle of each nest. Then pop a few chocolate eggs into each well and place the nests in the fridge to set.

Auntie's Classic Movie Club

Sometimes, as much as an aunt wants to be an action hero full of great ideas for wacky and wild things to do, she just needs a bit of a sit down. Luckily, sometimes nieces and nephews do too. If it's a wet Sunday afternoon and the only thing that seems exciting is cosying up on the sofa with a big bowl of freshly popped popcorn, a blanket and a good movie to watch, here are some never-fail classics that all the family will love:

THE LION KING (1994)

This is a Disney favourite with songs written by Elton John and Tim Rice that has every family member crooning along to 'The Circle of Life'. With all the wild animals that make up the cast, theatrical nieces and nephews will enjoy imitating monkeys, hippos and lions with all the matching noises. This film has moments that will make you giggle, sing, gasp and even shed a tear or two. But don't worry, there is a happy ending.

THE TOY STORY FILMS (1995-2010)

Pioneers of CGI animation, the *Toy Story* movies ask what toys would get up to if they could walk and talk when no one was around. The answer seems to be plenty of comedy and chaos! Follow the antics of Woody, Buzz and their motley crew of playthings as they do all they can to keep a place in their owner Andy's toy box.

FAMOUS AUNTS

Emma Roberts is a young actress in Hollywood who's beginning to make a splash. She's been in lots of movies and TV shows, all at just eighteen. But there was always a good chance she'd turn out to be a talented actress with an aunt like Julia. Julia Roberts's family is full of great actors and Emma is weary of people thinking it's a case of celebrity nepotism: 'I think there are a lot of people out there who say the really low blow of "She's just in the business because of her family." I do it because I love to do it. There have been a lot of parts I've been up for that I haven't gotten . . . I'm just being myself and doing what I want to do. I'm having a lot of fun.' The two actresses bear a strong family resemblance and for the first time have performed in the same movie together, *Valentine's Day*.

LEMONY SNICKET'S A SERIES OF UNFORTUNATE EVENTS (2004)

Most definitely a black family comedy with lots of chaotic peril at every turn, this film has something for everyone. The Baudelaire children lose their parents in a mysterious house fire and are sent to live with the strange and selfish Count Olaf, who makes no bones about only wanting them for their inheritance. They cleverly plot their escape and stay with other still-strange but much lovelier relatives like woolly Aunt Josephine who's pretty much scared of her own shadow. Not the sort of fearless auntie that we're all used to! Perhaps the message here is to do everything Aunt Josephine *wouldn't* do.

THE WIZARD OF OZ (1939)

This timeless piece of cinematic history has Judy Garland as the sweet-as-pie Dorothy who is whisked from her real life in Kansas to the magical Land of Oz by a huge tornado. Luckily she has her faithful dog Toto by her side as she sings and dances her way to meet the Wizard, in the hope he can send her home again. The much-loved heart-warming tunes 'Somewhere Over the Rainbow', 'We're Off to See the Wizard' and 'If I Only Had a Brain' will get everyone using their vocal chords. As fun as Oz can be, Dorothy knows she must get home to her beloved Aunt Em – one of the best movie aunts out there! If you can inspire this much devotion as an aunt, then you're definitely on the right track.

Agony Aunt

An aunt can have all the age and wisdom of a parent, but also provide the understanding and sympathy of a friend – an excellent aunt knows how to get the best of both worlds. That's why children find it easier talking to an aunt about their problems, rather than their parents or a teacher. A good aunt is always ready to supply whatever kind of help her nieces and nephews need, even if it's just by listening. Most problems you'll hear about will boil down to the child wanting to be reassured that they're not alone and that everyone experiences a similar thing at one time or another.

Don't hold back on sharing your own childhood experiences if you think it will help. If you haven't been through something like it, be positive and supportive and give them lots of hugs and squeezes. Everyone needs to have a cry and get negative feelings out of their system now and again – even wise old aunts – so stay away from phrases like 'there's no use crying over spilled milk' and 'sleep on it and you'll feel differently in the morning'. Give them your undivided attention – switch off the TV, sit side by side on the sofa, and clear everyone else out as subtly as you can – then swear on your life that whatever they tell you will go no further. Here are some subjects that are common hurdles for children as they grow up.

HOW CAN I MAKE SOMEONE MY FRIEND?

Younger children may ask for your advice on making friends, especially when they're new at school or move to a different area. Of course it will break your heart to think your niece or nephew is all alone, but don't show any of this worry to them. It's important to help them remain confident.

Remember when friendships were made and broken as often as the lunch bell rang? It's entirely natural that there will be times when they don't have a huge gang of close friends. If they are shy and need encouragement, why not suggest they start talking to someone in their class about one of their hobbies? Do they like a particular sport or TV show? Suggest that they try asking new friends about their skills and see if they have any in common that they can practise together in the playground.

The key thing is to reassure the child that they are fun, interesting and that anyone would be mad not to want to be their friend. A little confidence goes a long way, so just tell them how much you love hanging out with them because they're so cool. They may tell you that you 'don't count' because you're an auntie, but they'll take it to heart.

DO SAY: 'I used to be shy at school, but then I asked some girls if I could join their hopscotch game and we became great pals. It was hard at first, but it was worth it.'

DON'T SAY: 'Offer them your best toy to play with, or your lunch money.'

THERE'S SOMEONE AT SCHOOL WHO ISN'T VERY NICE TO ME . . .

Children of all ages are affected by bullying and it can be the very hardest thing about growing up. The first thing to establish when your niece or nephew tells you that they're being bullied is whether they've told a teacher or their parents. They may be scared to and beg you not to tell them either, but if they are in real danger of being physically or emotionally hurt then it's your duty to protect them. Talk to their parents, explain what's going on and discuss how they can become involved without the child knowing that you've leaked their secret.

Not all bullying is serious enough to involve other authorities, so use your best judgement and if you're in any doubt, share the problem with other aunties or your siblings.

If your niece or nephew is getting in trouble for fighting back against the bully or bullies, then try and give them some coping mechanism for when they feel frightened and under stress. The first step is always to walk away from a bully and ignore them. If the bullies can't be avoided, suggest taking three big breaths and letting each one out slowly. Tell them not to rise to any taunts but instead they should imagine a big brick wall between them and the bullies that horrible words can't get through. Explain that bullies are people who feel very unhappy about themselves, and that's why they take it out on others. Instead of feeling angry towards a bully they should feel sorry for them because they aren't a very happy person inside. Above all, do tell your niece and nephew that there is *absolutely* nothing wrong with them, that they are wonderful and amazing and that they should come to you the minute they feel unhappy about the situation.

DO SAY: 'You don't need this mean person as a friend so just walk away and don't look back. A mean person isn't worth your time or even thinking about.'

DON'T SAY: 'Well, be mean to them back then!'

HOW DO YOU TALK TO SOMEONE YOU HAVE A CRUSH ON?

Admitting to a first crush can be the absolute height of embarrassment when you're a teenager, so an aunt should refrain from any sort of cheeky smile or wink when they hear this news. Instead, take it just as seriously as if one of your adult friends had brought their relationship dilemmas to you. If your niece and nephew can't quite get the courage together to speak to their crush, help them rehearse a few conversational topics and questions, and come up with a plan of when they could talk to the object of their affections. Do they walk home from school along the same route? Maybe your niece or nephew could suggest a group outing to the cinema so they don't have the pressure of initiating an actual 'date'. Give them the secret to all good conversations: asking questions. Everybody loves talking about their own hobbies, families and memories, so all the besotted teen has to do is pick a few leading questions and then try and control their blushing when their crush talks.

If your niece or nephew has been turned down then be sympathetic and share a story of when you've been unlucky in love. This should make them see that it's something that

happens to everyone and it's not the end of the world. In a week they'll most likely be bringing you news of a new 'the one'.

DO SAY: 'Just try and get to know them; they'll see how great you are once they start talking to you.'

DON'T SAY: 'Ooooooooooooooh! You've got a crush! You've got a crush!'

EVERYONE ELSE IS DOING IT BUT ME . . .

Peer pressure can affect children of all ages. Smaller children may be under peer pressure to act up at school and not be seen as a 'nerd', while teens may feel pressure to try cigarettes or alcohol. It takes courage to stand out from the crowd, so do everything you can to show your niece or nephew that following the pack isn't always the best idea. Advise them that, when they're in a situation where friends are telling them to do something, they should stop, take a deep breath and think 'Would I do this if they weren't here?'. If the answer is no, then they should just walk away. Real friends will accept you for who you really are, not who they want you to be, after all. Independence is a great trait to encourage, as it will give your nieces and nephews lots of courage and confidence in later life.

DO SAY: 'I understand what it's like to be curious, but there are side effects you should know about . . .'

DON'T SAY: 'I'm so disappointed that you'd even think of doing that.'

MUM AND DAD ARE BEING SO UNFAIR!

Children may well see you as a neutral middle ground when they fall out with their parents. Try and gently point out how they can resolve the conflict with Mum and Dad and smooth things over. Encourage them to keep calm and apologize if they've been a bit stroppy. Make it clear you see their side of things too, but explain that to make a family work everyone needs to compromise now and then.

If you're caught in the crossfire of a squabble amongst nephews and nieces then being neutral is pretty much essential. Don't get drawn into who started it or whose fault it is. State very simply that you're not interested in who started the argument, just who's going to be mature enough to end it so you can all go back to having a good time.

DO SAY: 'Enough squabbling. Now, who wants to beat me at Wii tennis?'
DON'T SAY: 'No one said life was fair.'

> 'It is no use telling me that there are bad aunts and good aunts. At the core they are all alike. Sooner or later, out pops the cloven hoof.'
>
> BERTIE WOOSTER, IN *THE CODE OF THE WOOSTERS* BY P. G. WODEHOUSE (1881–1975)

FAMOUS AUNTS

Family relations can be tricky things that require careful diplomacy. This is true of families today *and* families throughout history. Aunts can be a little self-serving at times, but can still act for the good of their nieces and nephews. A famous historical example is that of Anne Boleyn and her sister Mary's child, Henry Carey. Mary had been a mistress of Henry VIII *before* Anne Boleyn set her cap at marrying him. Anne may have usurped her sister's place with the king, but she made sure that Mary was taken care of after her husband died and left her with large debts, *and* paid for nephew Henry to be well educated.

Action Aunt

If you're blessed with buckets of energy and fall into the Outdoorsy Auntie category (see page 22) then your siblings will absolutely love you for taking your nieces and nephews off their hands for an afternoon or a weekend. Here are some great ideas for action-packed adventures, both home and away.

OUT AND ABOUT

The adventure playground

If your nieces and nephews are energetic, then an adventure playground will suit them down to the ground. Do some Internet research or contact your local tourist information office to find an adventure park near you. Pack a healthy picnic before you set off, with lots of fruit and bottles of water. With plenty of climbing frames, monkey bars and zip wires to clown about on, you just need to let the kids loose and point them towards the giant slides.

Let the children charge around to their hearts' content, getting plenty of good exercise and fresh air, until the clouds gather or the park starts to close. Then you'll have a quiet, exhausted troop to take back home in blissful silence.

A day at the coast

The seaside doesn't have to be all flashy piers and clouds of candyfloss; you can head to a quieter coastal town and take in the fresh air and beautiful surroundings. The sea's natural beauty and changing landscape often attracts artists so you might happen upon lots of small art shops or galleries as you explore. There'll be plenty of wildlife to examine, so before your trip borrow a book about fish and sea life from your local library and arm yourself with some small nets and empty glass jars. Take your nieces and nephews on a ramble along the beach and examine the seaweed, rock pools and shells you come across. If you can scoop up any specimens in the glass jars, it will make your observations easier, but make sure to put them back again. You can explain to your nieces and nephews how important it is not to disturb ecosystems, even on the tiniest scale, as all living things affect each other.

At the theme park

This is the ideal way to entertain teenagers for a day, especially stroppy ones. Double-check with their parents before you leave that they're happy for them to have a couple of hours to wander about on their own. Then explain to your nieces and nephews that you're going to spend the first few hours together, have a small 'do your own thing' break and then meet at an agreed time and spend the rest of the day as a group again. This will mean you get lots of good bonding time when you can scream and giggle at all the rides together, but it also means that they get to blow off some steam without the olds around.

Just make sure they have your mobile phone number to hand. Otherwise, plonk yourself down in a cafe and have some quality aunt time with a good book and a coffee. Then get the energy levels pumping up again as you band together for your final dash around the park. A handy hint for practical aunts: take a few healthy snacks and bottles of water. Planning in advance means you can save your nieces and nephews from junk food and save your pockets from being emptied . . . If you're going on a sunny day, take hats and sunscreen.

On a nature trail

Do some research about your local area and locate your nearest leafy park, nature reserve or public gardens. Look for somewhere that has its own nature trails for you to follow and guides to what sort of flora and fauna to watch out for. Kit yourself and your young explorers out in sturdy walking boots or trainers and waterproof jackets, and take a bag with lots of drinks and snacks to keep your trekking team full of beans. Take some handy face wipes too, so that if anyone gets their hands mucky investigating the undergrowth you can clean up on the spot – it's not likely there'll be a sink nearby! If you're not that well versed on your flora and fauna, take along a book about wildlife so you can all take turns identifying what you've seen and learn all sorts of interesting facts.

If the park you're going to doesn't have any nature trails of its own then, to give more of a structure to your adventure, prepare a list of things to hunt down: the leaves from different trees, flowers, insects and birds. Your nieces and nephews can tick off each find as they go along and anything that interests them can be looked up on the Internet or in an encyclopaedia when you all get home. If you're feeling a little cheeky and really want to run them ragged, why not add

a made-up, strange-sounding animal to the list? After ten minutes of walking in circles and puzzled looks you can admit the truth and hope they've found it as funny as you have.

ON HOME TURF

The obstacle race

On a lovely bright day, make the most of the sunshine and get the partygoers out in the fresh air. Forage about for any outside toys – balls, skipping ropes, hula hoops, Frisbees and even a garden flowerpot or two if you're lacking in toys. Use these items to invent a simple obstacle course of things to jump over, run around, wriggle under and through, or throw and catch. Get the children to help design the course, based on whatever sports or athletics they're particularly fond of.

When the course is ready, each child (and grown-up, for that matter – no spectators allowed) races through as fast as they can while you time them on your watch and cheer encouragement. Let them have as many attempts as they like – ideally until they're completely tuckered out. Your nieces and nephews will also really enjoy seeing you jog your way along the course, and you'll have to accept any giggling at your sporting skills or lack thereof with good grace. Tidy up the garden together when it's time to go in and then unwind like all good athletes with a glass of milk and an apple to restore some energy.

Give your course the Olympic feel by including 'marathon' long laps around the garden, a standing long jump and a gymnastic forward roll. If you're a crafty aunt, you could even throw together a cheap and cheerful medal for each child taking part using metallic wrapping paper or kitchen foil. If you're a musical aunt, you could even get everyone singing or humming the national anthem as you award the medals.

SPECIAL AUNT STORIES

Dustin Hicks lives in Lubbock, Texas, but in 2009 he started an action-packed journey of more than a thousand miles – on foot. He started this mammoth run in aid of his favourite aunt, Debbie, who suffers from lymphoma. Dustin was deserted by his road crew and came down with the flu, but still refused to give up his run across three states, carrying everything he needed on his back and relying on local sponsors to give him food, water and shelter. This real-life Forrest Gump said, 'It would have made a lot of sense to simply pack up and go home, but I'm stubborn and proud.' His goal was to raise a million dollars for cancer research, all in aid of his beloved Aunt Debbie.

~~~~~~

Great games for the local park

What's the time, Mr Wolf?

This playground classic is a great game to use up tons of youthful energy – and auntie energy, come to that. To demonstrate the game, take up the role of Mr Wolf for the first turn. Stand at one end of the garden or playing field with your back to the kids and your hands over your eyes. Nieces and nephews should stand in a line at the other end, facing your back. In a chorus, they should shout, 'What's the time, Mr Wolf?' Then you, as Mr Wolf, shout a time. If you say, 'Three o'clock,' all the children must take three big steps forward, counting them as they go. The kids keep asking Mr Wolf the same question, until you shout 'Dinnertime!' The minute you shout this, turn around and chase the children back to their starting line. They have to scream and run away from you to avoid being caught. If you do catch someone then they become the new Mr Wolf. If your nieces and nephews are just too darn quick, go back to your position and start the game again.

Stuck in the mud

Everyone who's ever set foot in a playground will be very familiar with tag (or tig, as it's also known) but Stuck in the mud is an interesting twist on a childhood classic. You still start with someone who's 'It' and they then chase all the other players around to try and tap them with their hand. If a player is caught, they become 'stuck' and must freeze on the spot with their arms out like an aeroplane and their legs apart. The player who is 'It' is aiming to stick everyone in the mud, but the tricky part is this: all the players as yet unstuck can unstick someone by crawling between their legs. Then they are free once more!

~~~~~~

A tactically minded 'It' may hang around those that are stuck to catch any heroic-feeling players, but others may just choose to run round like a headless chicken till they've caught everyone. This game is guaranteed to end in lots of happy, breathless kids.

'First the sweetheart of the nation, then the aunt, woman governs America because America is a land of boys who refuse to grow up.'

SALVADOR DE MADARIAGA Y ROGO,
SPANISH DIPLOMAT (1886–1978)

$\mathscr{H}$alloween $\mathscr{S}$creams

Halloween is the time of year when a fun aunt can really let her naughty side show, whether it's coming up with the most gruesome outfits for her nieces and nephews or planning clever little tricks to surprise them. Here are some ideas to have a truly ghoulish time.

TRICK OR TREAT?

Whether you're anticipating the neighbourhood kids dropping by to show off their spookiest costumes and collect some treats or playing host to just your nieces and nephews on Halloween, it's worth doing a little bit of groundwork around the house and preparing some games to really chill those spines . . .

Balloons of doom!

Despite a little messy (but enjoyable) preparation and cleaning up afterwards, this is a very fun game with an element of risk to it. This is best played out in the garden or in a garage if the weather isn't very amenable.

CRRRRRRRRRRRRRRRRRRRRRRRR

YOU WILL NEED: Dark-coloured balloons, a blindfold, water, a jug, a funnel, glitter, small individually wrapped sweets, pins, some string.

HOW TO PREPARE: Before your devilish guests arrive, take out your balloons. Fill your jug with water and use it to pour roughly a cup of water into about a third of the balloons. The funnel will come in handy at this point. Then blow these balloons up until full-sized and tie off the ends. Put these carefully to one side. You've just made your booby traps.

Add a hefty handful of glitter to the water remaining in the jug. Take a further third of the balloons and fill each one up with just a little water. Blow them up and tie the ends. These are your decoys.

Take the last balloons and pop two or three small sweets into each one. Then blow them up until full-sized, and tie off. These are the prizes your spooky guests will be hunting.

Just before the party arrives, use some string to tie up each balloon at the head height of the children. If you are outside, a tree's branches are an ideal place to hang the balloons, or you could use a garden trellis. If you are in a garage or shed, you could tie them to a broom handle and then hold this up with another adult holding the other end. The idea is to form a sort of bunch or curtain of balloons hanging down, close to each other.

When the children arrive keep the lights dim and explain to them that the balloons of doom hold mysterious prizes to those who are brave . . . The children can take it in turns to be led blindfolded to the balloons, then spun around several times so they can randomly pick which one to pop with the pin. They might be lucky and find some sweets, or they might be extremely unlucky and get a little soggy in the

CRRRRRRRRRRRRRRRRRRRRRRRR

process. Keep going until all the balloons are popped or everyone is too wet to carry on. If a few of the children didn't find any sweets at all then reward them with some at the end, for being extra brave. Make sure to clear up the water before too long, so no one is in danger of slipping. And make sure you don't get roped into playing next time!

Monsters from the deep . . .

If you want to help your nieces and nephews prepare a 'trick' to take with them on their trick-or-treating or if you want to lure them into a little trick of your own, it doesn't take much more than a few household supplies and a gruesome imagination . . .

YOU WILL NEED: Several Tupperware containers or empty ice cream tubs; hard-boiled eggs; tinned spaghetti; a tin of custard; plastic spiders, snakes etc.; scissors; tea towels or serviettes.

HOW TO PREPARE: This will be a game to test your young Frankensteins' bravery and to really play on the idea that if you can't *see* something you can still be extremely scared of it!

In one tub mix the shelled boiled eggs (make sure to keep them whole) with the custard. Don't worry – this is not to be eaten! This will be your 'Cyclops' eyeballs in slime' when it's time for the kids to have a feel. In another tub empty out the tin of spaghetti (hoops don't work so well for this, so make sure you use just long strands) and throw in the plastic spiders and snakes, if you have them. This will be your tub of 'Flesh-eating worms and poisonous beasts'. With another tub, carefully cut out a hole in the bottom that is big enough to get your whole hand and wrist through.

Before your guests descend, line up the three tubs (or however many you can dream up as a wicked witch aunt for the night – anything goes as long as it feels icky and weird) on a table and drape a tablecloth or serviette over each one. Put on your best dramatic serious face as you welcome the children into your hall of horrors. Do they dare put their hands into these cages of monsters from the deep? If they do, riches (or sweets) await them . . .

As you introduce the children to the foul contents of each tub by its imaginative name, make sure to get them to close their eyes. Then, as they touch each one and squeal as the contents squelch beneath their fingers, move them to the final tub – the one with the hole in the bottom. Tell them this is the most ferocious creature of all – a blood-sucking leech. While they have their eyes closed, pick up the tub and slip your hand into the hole cut in the bottom. As the child nervously puts their hand inside, wait a few seconds then grab their hand with your own. If you don't get a round of screams then your nieces and nephews are made of very stern stuff.

Bobbing for apples

This classic game won't fail to keep your nieces and nephews entertained on Halloween – if a little bit wet.

YOU WILL NEED: A large bucket or basin, water, a stopwatch and lots of apples.

HOW TO PREPARE: Rinse out your bucket thoroughly before you start preparations for the game – especially if it was last used for cleaning the car. Fill it with cool, but not too cold, water and drop in the apples. The apples will float on the surface, ready to be 'bobbed'. Each player must put their hands behind their backs and dip their face into the water to try and snap up an apple with their teeth. A lot harder than it sounds. Use your stopwatch to record how long it takes each player to snare themselves an apple and the winner will be the player with the fastest time. Keep lots of towels handy so that players can dry themselves after their bobbing and do make sure you are especially vigilant with young children. Don't leave children unattended with the water, just as a precaution.

Don't expect to be left out of the bobbing just because you're the organizer, but do spare a thought for poor grannies present who may have dentures . . .

SCARY MOVIES FOR TEENS

If you're spending time with some teen nephews and nieces on Halloween and you think they're a bit too old for putting white sheets over their heads and knocking on doors for chocolate bars, then why not rely on some tried and trusted and truly terrifying scary movies to provide the entertainment? Here are some chilling classics (but do make sure to check with their parents first that they're happy for you all to watch these).

Gremlins (1984)

This movie is a diabolical mix of mirth, mayhem and terrifying monsters – perfect for the little monsters in your life at Halloween! Young Billy is brought home the cutest pet by his dad one Christmas: the fluffy but strange Gizmo. But, being a normal teenager, Billy forgets to take care of his new pet by the rules. When he feeds Gizmo after midnight and pours water on him accidentally, he inadvertently unleashes a whole swarm of green, scaly, mischievous gremlins on his small hometown. In a flash, the gremlins are creating Christmas chaos in their bid for world domination. Can Billy rid his town of them completely? Here's a clue: there's a sequel, *Gremlins 2: The New Batch* . . .

A Nightmare on Elm Street (1984)

This is for the really brave (and it was given an eighteen certificate so make sure you get the OK from the parents first). Perhaps one of the most recognizable ghoulish 'baddies' on film, Freddy Kruger turned up to scare the wits out of teenagers in the eighties with his scarred face, razor-sharp fingered gloves and trademark stripy jumper. Nancy and her friend realize they're having the same nightmares and, what's worse, some of the neighbourhood kids are starting to die in their sleep. Can the bogeyman they're dreaming of be murdering them as they snooze? There's only one way to stay alive on Elm Street: stay awake! This modern classic spawned a whole line of sequels and follow-ons, so why not have a whole marathon of Freddy films? If the aunt in question is brave enough, of course . . .

The Others (2001), starring Nicole Kidman and Christopher Ecclestone

This film is a masterpiece in jumpy terror – not for the faint-hearted by any means. Nicole Kidman is the very proper and anxious Grace, mother to two children allergic to sunlight. She keeps their house, in misty Jersey, shrouded in darkness with heavy curtains and blinds. But the darkness hides all sorts of chilling secrets, strange noises and unexplainable happenings . . . Is the house haunted, as Grace fears? When a psychic is brought in to find these mysterious spirits, Grace discovers the truth in one of the most shocking twists in movie history. If any of your party guess it they deserve a very big bag of sweets indeed! Turn the lights out and prepare to be spooked.

ccccccccccccccccccccccccccccccc

COSTUMES FIT FOR A GHOUL

You don't need to spend lots of money on Halloween costumes for the children in your life, not if you're the sort of crafty, resourceful aunt who can always make a little go a long way. Just thinking of new ways to use household objects and every-day clothing can save the scary day when you have to rustle up a costume in a flash. These few ideas are tried and tested over generations of trick-or-treaters.

Zombie

Perhaps the simplest of all costumes to throw together in a hurry, a zombie can also be the spookiest. To recreate the look of the living dead, you'll need some old clothes; dark grey or black eyeshadow; scissors; cornflour and some acting tips. Make sure you have permission from the kids' parents before you start to make small tears and rips in the clothes with the scissors, just in case they need to be saved for another day. You're going for the look of a ghoulish zombie who's risen from the grave, so give the children big, dark circles of eye-shadow to create a hollow-eyed skeleton feel. Sprinkle their hair and clothes liberally with the cornflour and rub it in so they look like dusty corpses come to life. Pat some lightly on their faces too. Now, give a quick lesson in making zombie groans and walking in a slow, lumbering shuffle. The children will go from rosy-cheeked innocents to stone-cold monsters in no time.

ccccccccccccccccccccccccccccccc

Werewolf

If you have nieces and nephews that are as energetic and boisterous as excited puppies then why not let them take a walk on the wild side this Halloween? With a little forward planning and some clever adjustments to everyday things, you'll soon have a pack of werewolves ready to unleash on the neighbourhood. You'll need a few metres of fake fur material, available from haberdasheries and craft shops; scissors; a needle and thread; plastic scary teeth from a joke or costume shop; a hat and pair of gloves for each child. Cut two large ear shapes out of the fur and stitch these onto either side of the hat – don't worry if you're not a great sewer, very simple stitches will do here and messy ones won't show. Cut a long, thin strip of the fur and attach it to the top of the child's trousers or skirt with a few more stitches: this will be the tail. Cut two rough squares of fur and sew these onto the sections of the gloves that cover the back of the hand – these will transform the children's hands into monstrous hairy claws. If you're an arty aunt or good with make-up, you could lightly draw some whiskers with a brown or black eyeliner pencil on their cheeks, then pop in the plastic teeth to complete the canine look. Let's just hope there isn't a full moon . . .

Spider

As long as you don't have too big a fear of spiders yourself, you can have great fun putting together this creepy crawly outfit. You'll need two pairs of old black tights; yesterday's newspaper; scissors; a needle and thread or sticky tape; a black

T-shirt and trousers for each child. Cut the two legs from each pair of tights and stuff them with balled-up sheets of newspaper. This will make four extra limbs to go with the child's original set of four, to give an eight-legged appearance. Once the legs are full of paper either stitch them or tape them to the T-shirt, equally spaced underneath the sleeves with two on each side. *Voilà!* A little arachnid in your own home.

A VERY SCARY SNACK: TOFFEE APPLES

Toffee apples are a classic treat for the Halloween festival and it's as much fun to make them at home as it is to crunch into them as you make the rounds of trick-or-treating.

YOU WILL NEED:
> 8 apples
> 8 wooden ice lolly sticks
> 170 g (6 oz) fruit sugar
> 120 ml (4¼ fl. oz) water
> 1 tsp cider vinegar
> 1 tbsp golden syrup
> 30 g (1¼ oz) butter
> Hundreds and thousands

Makes 8

① Line a baking tray with greaseproof paper.

② Carefully wash each apple in warm water, then dry with a tea towel.

③ Holding the apple so that the stalk is facing you, insert an ice lolly stick into the apple as close to the stalk as you can.

④ Add the fruit sugar, water, cider vinegar, golden syrup and butter to a pan and place on the hob at a medium heat. Once the butter has completely melted and the sugar has dissolved, turn up the heat. Let the liquid simmer for five minutes; it should turn a lovely golden-brown colour and have a syrupy consistency.

⑤ Remove the pan from the heat and leave it to cool on a heat-resistant surface for a few minutes.

⑥ Pick up an apple by its stick and dip it into the pan so that it gets covered by the syrup. Repeat this with all the apples.

⑦ Sit the apples on the baking tray with the sticks pointing upwards. Sprinkle with hundreds and thousands. Leave to set.

On the
First Day of Christmas,
My Auntie
Gave to Me . . .

An aunt with plenty of Christmas cheer will not only be popular during the festive season, but will prove herself very useful too, especially when the school holidays roll around. Mum and Dad will have lots on their plate – preparing for big family feasts and helping Santa find the right truckload of presents to deliver on Christmas Eve – so an aunt can step in and provide lots of fun and distracting activities for the children of the family. Christmas games and tasks are perfect for keeping excited little people busy while the grown-ups toil away with wrapping paper and sticky tape. Plus, children love to feel like they're involved in making family occasions special and they'll enjoy doing their bit. Here are some very Christmassy ideas to get you started . . .

DECK THE HALLS

There are lots of quick, easy and budget-friendly ways to decorate the family home at Christmas. You just need a few key materials, some crafty assistants and lots of Christmas spirit!

Popcorn strings

A traditional classic, this is a great activity for a wet and miserable December afternoon when you have some bored nieces and nephews to entertain. Pop lots of popcorn in the microwave, carefully following the instructions on the packet. Get some long lengths of string and thread them onto thick, blunt needles – you can find these in the wool section of your local haberdashery. Tie a big knot at the end of each string and get comfy as you sit down with the kids to thread on pieces of popped popcorn to make lovely garlands for the tree or for hanging around the house. If some popcorn ends up being munched as you go, you can look the other way.

Crackers that go with a bang

Buy a kit to make and decorate your own crackers during the festive period. Your nieces and nephews will have a great time colouring in, painting and adding stickers to the crackers, as well as deciding what little treats to add as prizes. Save the handmade crackers for the table on Christmas Day, so the kids can feel they've really contributed to the big day.

Handle with care

If you have access to a garden or have a wooded park or forest nearby, why not collect some very festive holly and ivy? Deck out the children (and yourself, of course) in gardening gloves that will protect hands from the spikier side of holly. Take some garden scissors and a bag to collect what you find. Gather together bunches of your festive foliage and tie them up with red or tartan ribbon. These will look lovely either hanging on the door in place of a wreath or laid on the dining table as a centrepiece. You can even tie on some tinsel or baubles to really add a touch of Christmas glamour.

Last Christmas, I gave you my card

A very simple way to absorb children for a few hours is with any Christmas cards you may have been given last year. You can either cut out any good images or words from these cards yourself – robins, snowmen, gifts, plus words like 'Noel' and 'Jingle Bells' – or get your nieces and nephews to help. Then you could make one big Christmas collage by gluing the shapes and words on a large piece of card or even wrapping paper. Or you could make new Christmas cards by folding over pieces of A4 card, sticking recycled card shapes on the front and writing inside.

Chain reaction

If you've been busy wrapping and have lots of odds and ends of wrapping paper left over, don't automatically put these in the recycling box – they can be reborn as a lovely paper chain. Cut the scraps into strips of equal width and roughly the same length. Then get your helpers together in a circle and each bend one strip of paper round into a loop and glue the ends together. The next strip is put through this loop before being secured to form a loop itself. Carry on this way until you use up all the Christmassy paper and have a colourful paper chain or two to drape over the tree or over the top of a picture frame, mantelpiece or mirror.

ALL FUN AND GAMES

Christmas wouldn't be Christmas without some family games, but it can be tricky to find something that will keep all ages entertained. Don't be worried if you stick to games that you played when you were little – those classics are still around for a reason. Drag the children away from their computer games and MP3 players to show them how you would entertain yourselves in the *olden days* . . .

● Everybody enjoys a game of charades (especially aunties who've had a festive tipple or two!) but during the Christmas holidays why not give them a seasonal spin by sticking to Christmas songs, films, food and stories? With 'Jingle Bells', 'A Christmas Carol', roast turkey, Christmas pudding and 'The Twelve Days of Christmas', it'll be very late before you run out of Christmas items to mime.

- Past generations might have stood around a piano and sung Christmas carols, but you can still have a singalong without the baby grand (or indeed any musical talent whatever). Stick to simple tunes like 'We Wish You a Merry Christmas' and 'Jingle Bells' and buy a compilation of Christmas songs as a backing track. Flat notes can also be concealed by singing 'in the round'. Divide your assembled family into three groups. The first group start singing and the second group join in at the second line, but singing the first. The third group join in after another line, again singing the first line. This is great fun and can either create a lovely effect, or be a complete din – but either way it's guaranteed to entertain.

- If you have invested in a Christmas compilation CD you can also put together a quick and easy game of 'Guess that song'. Play well-known Christmas carols and pop songs from your compilation on your stereo and pause them after the first few notes. Your teams have to identify the song title and can write down their answers or just shout them out, depending on how much of a stickler for the rules you are.

- If charades has begun to get a bit tired, you can give a slight twist to the game and create fun out of thin air with a game of 'Invisible Sculptures'. Divide everyone into two teams – boys versus girls always seems to get competitive juices flowing. Tear up some sheets of scrap paper and get every player to write down three objects, on separate pieces, and pop them into a hat or bowl (this game will only work with objects, so save any film or book titles for charades – when

you can bear it again). One team member has a minute to stand in front of their team and communicate the words written on each piece of paper as they pull them out at random. Instead of straightforward miming, you have to 'mould' and 'sculpt' in the air to get across the word. Imagine you are a sculptor of invisible clay and run your hands over the object as you sculpt it and shape it and pull it. Make your actions big and bold so that your team can picture what it is you're sculpting. Keep taking it in turns to have a go until all the objects have been guessed.

- 'Flip the Kipper' is a fast, furious and very silly game – a perfect antidote to post-lunch lethargy. You'll need a stack of old newspapers, a pencil, scissors and string. Draw an outline of a fish (about 25 cm long) on one of the newspapers. Cut it out, going through enough sheets of paper to give a 'kipper' each to the whole family. Lay down string to mark start and finish lines at each end of the room. Line up your 'flippers' behind the starting line with a kipper on the floor in front of them and a rolled-up newspaper each. Ready, steady, go! Each racer has to beat their newspaper on the floor behind their kipper, to waft or 'flip' it along. The first fish over the finish line wins.

'I'm Charley's aunt from Brazil, where the nuts come from.'
FROM THE PLAY *CHARLEY'S AUNT* BY
BRANDON THOMAS (1856–1914)

FAMOUS AUNTS

Nieces and nephews always look to repay the generosity of their beloved aunts – though celebrities do it a little more lavishly than the rest of us! When American singing superstar Mariah Carey heard her aunt had fallen behind on a rent payment for her home in San Miguel, Venezuela she stepped in to help, not just paying off the debt, but also buying the entire property for her aunt.

STOCKINGS

Christmas wouldn't be Christmas without a stocking hung up for Santa to fill with lovely things. As a helpful aunt, why don't you offer to take responsibility for the stockings this year: it will mean one less parental responsibility for your sibling and a lot of fun for you. It will also remind you of the fun and thrill of delving into a stocking on Christmas morning and pulling out lots of entertaining gifts. It's not hard work and it doesn't have to be expensive, either. Here are some top tips for truly tantalizing stockings:

● Instead of buying a Christmas stocking from a store, why not buy some silly, long Christmassy socks or tights that will fit your niece or nephew and fill one of these with gifts. That way, the stocking itself becomes a handy gift – some toasty socks for cold December mornings. Roll up the other sock and tuck it in the toe of the stocking.

● You don't need to splash a lot of cash on stocking gifts, even if the kids are into flashy, brand-name toys this year. If they do worship one sort of toy in particular, why not track down some stationery with that branding or some stickers from that toy or TV show. Lots of big toys have their own collectable trading cards too.

● A handful of chocolate coins can provide all the sugary delight one stocking will need, so don't be tempted to go overboard on sweet treats. When the sugar crash kicks in that afternoon, no one will thank you for it. A few traditional clementines and a small box of raisins will make a tasty, healthy snack as the rest of the wrapping ripping commences . . . If you did want to include just one more indulgence, a square or two of Chewy, Crispy Bites (from page 131) wrapped up in kitchen foil and tinsel will satisfy your spoiling impulses and leave enough room for Christmas lunch.

● Great, absorbing gifts include a small bag of marbles, a pack of playing cards, a set of dominoes, a book of jokes or a quiz book, a magic trick or finger puppets – all of which will keep the kids amused while the adults have some time to themselves.

● If you have a glamorous niece then a few hair slides with flower details or pretend gemstones will keep her happy and busy.

- If you have a sporty nephew then a hacky sack (a small squishy ball) will keep him occupied in a quiet corner for a half hour or so.

- Party poppers, balloons and party whistles make fun additions and are also very cheap and cheerful.

- If you're a crafty aunt and have plenty of time in the run-up to Christmas you could track down a knitting pattern to knit some jolly, festive stockings or find a pattern to sew some using festively coloured materials with lots of ribbons and trimmings. It's always wonderful to have something made just for you, so a stocking with your nieces' and nephews' names sewn on will be just the ticket.

Aunties Between the Pages

If you're a culture vulture sort of aunt who prefers the written word to movies or TV, you can find plenty of aunts from between the pages of books, new and old. Some show great wisdom, great bravery and great skill, but some prove themselves to be great big idiots – so don't follow *all* the examples closely!

Betsey Trotwood in DAVID COPPERFIELD, Charles Dickens (1850)

Not the easiest of aunts, Betsey Trotwood's heart is still pretty much in the right place when it comes to taking care of poor orphan David Copperfield, after his stepfather has forced him to work in a bottle factory following the death of David's mother. Betsey shows, in fact, how far an aunt will go to put aside her own feelings for her young ward: she's not a great fan of boys or men – after some abysmal treatment from a useless husband – but when David really needs her, Betsey rescues him and provides for his education and later career.

Aunt Fanny Kirrin in the FAMOUS FIVE series, Enid Blyton (1942–1963)

Aunt Fanny is George's mother and is aunt to Anne, Dick and Julian. Throughout most of Enid Blyton's much-loved *Famous Five* books, Aunt Fanny is the strongest and central maternal figure. She is a wonderful old-fashioned pillar of aunt behaviour: always ready with kindness and care, a listening ear to news of any unfolding adventures and, of course, a jolly good picnic or two, with lashings of ginger beer, for the hungry Five.

Aunt Norris in MANSFIELD PARK, Jane Austen (1814)

Aunt Norris is most certainly a *bad* aunt. Always criticizing the novel's morally upright heroine Fanny, she is instead in awe of the more glamorous, but not so morally dependable, young characters and allows them to get away with all sorts of mischief. She's not a strict aunt, she's not a spoily aunt, she's not a cosy aunt – she's altogether useless! However, she does get her just desserts after allowing one of her nieces to behave rather scandalously; both Mrs Norris and her naughty niece Maria are shipped off to exile abroad, to be each other's punishment. A lesson to us all to pull our auntie socks up.

Aunt May in SPIDERMAN, Stan Lee and Steve Ditko (1962)

Comic books might not be everyone's idea of literature, but Aunt May is unarguably one of the best-known aunts on the planet. Peter Parker was orphaned as a young boy and then taken in by his Uncle Ben and Aunt May. May quickly became everything Peter could have wanted in an adoptive mother-figure: sweet, gentle and trusting. She's also amazingly resilient! Poor Aunt May has been kidnapped, attacked and threatened more times than a comic book fan can keep track of. Peter has to balance keeping her safe and protecting his secret identity.

Crafty Ideas

One of the best bits about being an aunt is indulging in that timeless joy of cutting, gluing, sticking and creating, which you probably last had time for at school. With your nephews and nieces around you, you can let your imagination run wild and inspire them to make all sorts of things. Even just looking inside the recycling boxes will start a journey of invention.

Here are a variety of ideas to keep little hands and minds busy over the holidays or the weekends they spend with their favourite aunt.

CARDS FOR EVERY OCCASION

Nephews and nieces love giving a special card on Mother's Day and Father's Day, and parents most certainly love receiving them, so why not help the children create something straight from the heart and totally original? Gather together any spare scraps of brightly patterned wrapping paper or wallpaper, plus any stickers or glitter to hand. If you have a digital camera, why not get really inventive and take some snaps of the children clowning about and pulling silly faces. Get these printed out and add them to your pile of materials.

Let the kids get stuck in and create whatever comes to mind. Keep them safe by monitoring the use of scissors (do the cutting yourself if the children are still little) and glue (as this can look too delicious to be left untasted by some children). The fun they will have getting messy will give you just as much of a warm glow as watching the moment when your siblings open the cards that have been made for them.

TOYS REALLY ARE CHILD'S PLAY

Sometimes the world of children's toys can feel like a non-stop stream of adverts for the latest big, shiny, expensive must-have and it's easy for an aunt to despair at not being able to compete. If you're watching your budget, but still want to wow your nieces and nephews with some truly special presents, why not make them something yourself? Take inspiration from whatever game is the child's absolute favourite at that moment and think of a small extra you could create yourself that would make that toy so much more fun. Here are some ideas to get you started but, just remember, it's the thought that counts.

- If they have a particular favourite film or TV show, why not try and customize some clothes to make them an outfit to emulate the main character? If your niece or nephew is mad for *Star Wars*, for example, you can get some very inexpensive hessian cloth and fashion together a robe, just like the Jedi wear. If you're not a dab hand at sewing, don't worry – your handy average office stapler can join bits of a thick material like this and make hems. Cut a long rectangle of the material that is longer than your niece or

nephew is tall by about 20 cm (8 inches). Join together the top two corners of the short end of the rectangle so that it forms a pointed hood – as if you were making the first folds of a paper aeroplane to make the nose of the plane. Then, just cut two armholes (they can be left very rough, if you like – after all, it's all about the Force). Expect lots of light sabre zooming noises and talk of Stormtroopers in this very special homemade outfit.

● Customize a cheap, plain T-shirt with fabric pens, buttons, sequins and any other embellishments you can get your hands on. Again, if sewing isn't your thing you can use special fabric glue to attach interesting details or just keep to fabric pens and illustrate the T-shirt with the child's name or a silly nickname. If the child is very young, make sure that anything to stick on is very securely attached, to avoid any chance of it coming loose and being swallowed.

If your niece or nephew is a member of a sports team, why not make up a whole stack of T-shirts in adult sizes so that every member of the family that wants to watch the next match or race can support them with slogans like 'Jack is the best' or 'Go Jack, Go!' (Once your niece or nephew hits adolescence they may find this more than a little bit embarrassing, so make the most of your opportunities before they turn thirteen.)

Teenagers might like customizing a pair of canvas sneakers. Pick up a cheap pair in a plain colour and let them go wild with the fabric pens and embellishments. Encourage them to try anything that comes to mind – who said shoes have to match anyway?

● If your niece or nephew is a big fan of board games and puzzles, there are some very simple and creative ways to make your own at home. For your very own board game, take 'Snakes and Ladders' as your inspiration. With some stiff card in a large square, draw on a grid of lines using a ruler, so that you are left with lots of boxes of the same size. Follow where the snakes and ladders are placed in the traditional family favourite – but here's where you can put your very own twist on things. If you have a niece or nephew who's mad about cars, why not change the ladders to motorways and the snakes to roadwork diversions? After numbering the squares as normal, you can then play with toy cars as counters. Similarly, you could give the game a jungle theme with tall trees to carry the counter up and the long neck of a giraffe to slide down again. You could stick green tissue paper leaves all around the outside of the board to add to the rainforest feel.

ARTY AUNTIES

If you're a crafty sort of aunt and an expert knitter, passing on your skill to the younger members of your family can be hugely rewarding. Don't worry if you can't tell your knits from your purls, though; you can still be a crafty sensation with your nieces and nephews. There are some fantastic beginners' knitting kits available from most department stores with a haberdashery section, and lots available online. They usually come with full instructions to explain the basics and contain all the wool and the needles you'll need. Alternatively, if you can just about pass on the basics, scarves are always a good

place to start. As well as being simple, you can use up any odds and ends of yarn you may have lying around to create fun and funky stripy scarves.

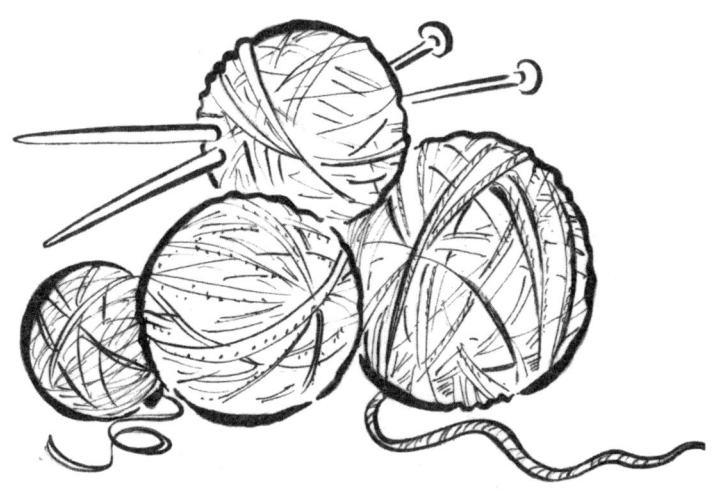

PLAY WITH IT AGAIN, SAM!

Sometimes the best fun comes from the simplest toys; if you've watched the kids of your family on Christmas Day put aside the most complicated, expensive toy in favour of the cardboard box it came in, you'll know just how baffling but true it is. So if you can't beat them, join them – encourage your nieces and nephews to make things out of recycled objects and just sit back and watch where their imagination will take them.

Cardboard boxes, cereal packets, toilet rolls and newspapers are great for cutting and sticking; toilet rolls can make excellent wheels or ships' funnels, cardboard boxes can become the cockpit of a plane or a little cottage, and torn-up newspapers combined with some watered-down non-toxic glue can make just about anything in fabulously sticky papier mâché. Plastic bottles and glass jars when washed out and clean are also really versatile and can kick-start all sorts of ideas: will they be rocket engines or swimming pools? Why not combine all of these things as you see fit to make a fairy-tale castle, a farmhouse or a spaceship? The hardest bit will be waiting for the papier mâché to dry so you can get creative with the paint.

Keeping Up With the Kids

One drawback to becoming an auntie is that you're frequently reminded that your own childhood is now behind you. But no matter how many decades have passed since you were listening to the pop charts and counting out your pocket money, you can still keep a tab on what's hot and what's not in the world of kids. The key thing here is to remember that children might not know as much as you, but they certainly know when someone's faking it. If you pretend to have seen their favourite band in concert twice or have met their favourite TV star in the supermarket you're more than likely to be found out in a flash. Don't be tempted to embellish on the truth to seem impressive, just gather the basic information and then ask *lots* of questions. Get your niece and nephew to fill you in on the rest by just opening up the conversation and you'll discover you're suddenly all clued up on modern culture and have had a lovely long chinwag with the kids in the process.

Doing just a little groundwork can reap big rewards and lots of brownie points from the nieces and nephews. Here are some places to start your detective work:

● Get down to the shops and pick up a few magazines aimed at teens. These will give you a good idea what sort of music, films, fashions and TV shows are being talked about now. It might also throw up some slang words that make absolutely no sense to you. The next time you're with your nieces and nephews, subtly use your collected research to start a conversation about what they're into at the moment. Be very honest and admit you've heard a new word you don't understand. They'll welcome the opportunity to teach you something for a change.

- Look up the top-ten album chart on the Internet for that week. Listen to a few tracks of one of the bestselling albums via a free music-sharing website such as Spotify and if you think it's enjoyable, ask the teens if they've heard it. Don't labour the point that it's 'cool' or they'll be very suspicious. Just be honest about what you think and discuss the music on an adult level. The teens will respect you for taking their tastes seriously, but might be tempted to giggle if you pretend it's what you have on your car stereo every day.

- If you come across new websites or technology in your teen research then use this as another great opener for the kids to explain something to you. They can show you how things work in plain language. Again don't pretend to know more than you do – let them be the experts for once. They'll love showing off to you about all the fancy gadgets they've tried.

- Reality TV might be your worst nightmare, but is almost universally popular with teens. Don't subject yourself to watching a whole series, but rather tell your nieces and

nephews that you've heard a lot about a show and you'd like to see what all the fuss is about. Sit through a Saturday night show with them with a bucket of popcorn and rate the acts or contestants as they appear. Well, that's the real point, isn't it?

● If there's a too-trendy-for-words clothes shop that your nieces and nephews love, don't put yourself through the torture of trying to pick them something really fashionable. Show that you've listened by buying them vouchers for that store when it comes to a birthday or Christmas, but be wise enough to know they're the only people who will really know what they want – and more importantly, what's cool.

Are You a PANK?

It may sound a bit odd, even slightly saucy, but you might just be a PANK – and without even realizing it. PANKs (or Professional Aunts No Kids) are now a force to be reckoned with in many modern families. A cool aunt who has her own career and a bevy of nieces and nephews – but as yet doesn't have children of her own – can play a vital role and save frazzled parents from headaches left, right and centre. While a parent has to think about loads of washing, homework deadlines and broken curfews, a PANK can focus on all the fun stuff: exciting days out, cinema trips with lots of popcorn and shopping for a cool new outfit. PANKs bring a little touch of glamour to family proceedings; with more time and disposable funds than the average parent, they're likely to turn up for Sunday lunch in a cool new trend, with expertly applied make-up and gorgeous new shoes, too. Little nieces will love their fashion sense and want to play dress-up in all their clothes.

And what could be more glamorous than a celeb PANK? The latest celebrity trend among famous, fabulous women is to throw themselves into being an aunt with the same enthusiasm they might usually save for a red carpet premiere. Celeb PANKs include Beyoncé, Kylie Minogue, Jessica Simpson, Miley Cyrus and Oprah Winfrey. They all love indulging their nieces and nephews, and are bursting with pride to welcome their siblings' new arrivals into the world.

If you think you might be setting the trends as a PANK already or suspect you're in need of a cool aunt makeover, take this quick test to see just how with it you really are.

QUESTION 1
  When you hear 'GaGa', what does it make you think of?

  A) Catchy pop tunes and bizarre but super-cool □
     outfits.
  B) Not a lot, but your best guess is an Italian □
     designer of some sort.
  C) A subtle way of saying someone is a bit loopy. □

QUESTION 2
  Where do you expect to see Gladiator sandals?

  A) On the catwalks and then in Topshop. □
  B) On Russell Crowe. □
  C) Nowhere – the Roman Empire was a long time □
     ago, silly.

QUESTION 3
  Where would you find Shia Le Boeuf?

  A) In a big Hollywood blockbuster. □
  B) On a French restaurant's menu. □
  C) Wherever you left it. □

QUESTION 4

Where did you get your mascara?

A) From the Chanel counter.
B) From a 2 for 1 offer at the chemist's.
C) What mascara?

QUESTION 5

How do you listen to your favourite music?

A) On my iPhone, of course, with the very latest apps.
B) My CD player hasn't broken yet, so I'm sticking to compact discs for now.
C) I play my LPs on a turntable, like a normal person.

QUESTION 6

What's your idea of a perfect day with your nieces and nephews?

A) Milkshakes and burgers at the bowling alley, then straight to the shopping mall for some essential accessories and beauty products – even for the nephews!
B) A good hearty stroll round the local park and maybe a DVD to snuggle up to afterwards.
C) A trip round the local history museum and then double-checking their homework until it's time for bed.

MOSTLY As:

You are just too cool for school, aren't you? A PANK through and through, you don't need any help in the style stakes. Carry on with the fabulous work, darling!

MOSTLY Bs:

You're almost there – being a PANK is in sight! Keep your eyes peeled and your ears open for new trends in music, fashion and movies. If you can bear not to be quite so sensible it would be a good start.

MOSTLY Cs:

Oh dear. I'm not sure you've got the hang of this. You need to read a whole stack of celebrity magazines and get yourself down to the beauty parlour, asap. Did anyone mention that it's now the twenty-first century?

Little Mouths to Feed

If there's one thing that unites children, it's an insatiable appetite for all things sweet. If you don't want to be a lazy aunt and simply dole out the same old chocolate bars as a snack, then get busy in the kitchen and whip up a few naughty treats now and then.

ROCKING ROCKY ROAD

YOU WILL NEED:

    75 g (2½ oz) mini marshmallows (or the same quantity of large marshmallows snipped into small pieces)
    75 g (2½ oz) digestive biscuits, broken up into pieces
    50 g (1¾ oz) glacé cherries, chopped into quarters
    50 g (1¾ oz) skinned almonds, chopped (optional)
    300 g (10½ oz) milk chocolate
    100 g (3½ oz) plain chocolate
    100 g (3½ oz) unsalted butter

Makes approx. 24 squares

① In a large mixing bowl combine the marshmallows, biscuit pieces, cherries and chopped almonds.

② Line a square baking tin with greaseproof paper.

③ On the hob, warm some water in a pan until it's boiling. Place a heatproof bowl over the pan so the steam rises to heat it. Break both kinds of chocolate into chunks and place them in the bowl.

④ Melt the chocolate until liquid and stir with a wooden spoon to mix the two kinds of chocolate together evenly. Carefully remove from the hob.

⑤ Add the dry ingredients to the bowl of chocolate and mix thoroughly.

⑥ Tip the mixture into the baking tin and, using the back of a spoon, press down until level.

⑦ Cover with cling film and put into the fridge to set.

⑧ When the mixture has set, cut into squares and tuck in.

CHEWY, CRISPY BITES

YOU WILL NEED:
200 g (7¼ oz) marshmallows
200 g (7¼ oz) hard toffees
1 large pack of Rice Krispies cereal

Makes approx. 24 squares

① Grease a deep square cake tin or dish.

② On the hob, warm some water in a pan until it's boiling. Place a heatproof bowl over the pan and add the marsh-mallows and toffees and stir until it's all melted into a delicious-looking goo.

③ Before the mixture starts to cool, quickly pour in the Rice Krispies and stir. This is when your little chefs come into their own as they use some serious elbow grease to stir furiously before the mixture starts to set.

④ Let the kids dollop out the sticky crispy mixture into the dish or tin, then press it down with the back of the spoon.

⑤ Cover with cling film and leave in the fridge to set. When it's set, turn the dish upside down and cut the slab into equal square pieces. These jaw-busting chewy but still crispy snacks will be an instant family favourite.

MERINGUE MESS

If you're after a super-quick pudding or sweet treat, this recipe is just the ticket. It involves crushing, mixing and eating. And that's it!

YOU WILL NEED:

6 mini meringue nests (1 per person)

1 punnet of strawberries

500 ml (17½ fl. oz) vanilla yoghurt

1 punnet of blueberries (or any other berries your nieces and nephews enjoy – the more fruit, the better!)

Serves 6

① In a large mixing bowl, crush the meringue nests with your hands or with a wooden spoon. Leave some medium-sized lumps for crunch and texture.

② Dollop in the yoghurt and combine with the meringue. Add the yoghurt a little at a time until all the meringue is covered, but before it gets too sloppy.

③ Spoon the mixture into bowls and sprinkle over the berries.

Serve and enjoy!

SPECIAL AUNT STORIES

An aunt with her wits about her really saved the day in the case of Jonathan Whitman. Just three years old, he decided to go for a walk on his own and so got lost in the woods in Attala County, Mississippi in 2009. His worried family started up a search party, but it was his aunt Tammy who went running when she heard his voice and quickly found him by spotting tracks he'd made through the woods. Aunt Tammy also had the wisdom to say that Jonathan would be on 'lockdown' from then on, to stop it ever happening again.

Glamour-puss Auntie

If you're a bit of a girly aunt or an aunt with just nieces in the family, then count your blessings and indulge in some really good girly bonding with a stay-at-home spa day. It's more fun than going to a professional spa and definitely more affordable. Here are some great tips for homemade beauty products that are quick and simple to mix up with your fellow gorgeous girls . . .

YUMMY YOGHURT AND STRAWBERRY FACE MASK

YOU WILL NEED:
   10 strawberries
   1 tbsp plain yoghurt
   2 tbsp honey

① Add the strawberries, yoghurt and honey to a bowl.

② Using a fork, mash all the ingredients together, leaving some small lumps of strawberry intact. You want to avoid the mixture becoming too runny as this will be difficult to apply to your skin.

③ Smooth the mask over clean skin. Relax for five minutes then wash off with warm water.

COOLING CUCUMBER FACE MASK

YOU WILL NEED:
   ½ cucumber, chopped and at room temperature
   90 g (3 oz) oatmeal
   2 tbsp plain yoghurt

① In a bowl, mix the cucumber and oats. Press the oats into the cucumber with the back of a wooden spoon so that they form a mushy paste.

② Add in the yoghurt and mix well.

③ Apply the mixture to clean skin, spreading evenly over the face and paying particular attention to covering oily patches.

④ Relax for 30 minutes while the mask cleanses and calms your skin.

⑤ Rinse off with lukewarm water and gently pat skin dry.

CREAMY AVOCADO FACE MASK

YOU WILL NEED:
  1 avocado
  1 tsp clear honey

① Use a sharp knife to slice the avocado around the stone. Open up the two halves, remove the stone and scrape out the meat from the skins with a spoon.

② In a bowl, mix together the flesh of the avocado and the honey. Use a fork so that the avocado mashes together with the honey evenly.

③ Apply the mixture to your face after a shower or bath. Leave it for 15–20 minutes.

④ Rinse off with lukewarm water, then gently pat your face dry with a towel.

BACK TO BEAUTY BASICS

It's not always appropriate to teach younger nieces about make-up and grown-up fashions. After all, childhood is short enough so aunts should help little girls stay little girls and enjoy the carefree fun that brings. Why not just teach your nieces about the basics of keeping your skin and hair clean, fresh and neat? These lessons will stay with them as they grow up and add make-up into their routine.

The skincare mantra

The first lesson you can pass on to little nieces is to cleanse, tone and moisturise. They may have enviably youthful skin now, but the best way to keep it soft and smooth as they grow is to look after it properly right from the very beginning.

Cleanse. When it comes to cleansing you can advise your nieces 'little and often'. A very mild, unperfumed soap is the 'little' and washing their face every night before bed is the 'often'. This routine will gently remove the dirt and old skin cells, but won't be too harsh and leave their skin feeling dry.

Tone. Young skin has lots of tone and elasticity, so toning isn't too tricky. The best way to tone up young skin is just to splash their face with cold water after cleansing or after a hot shower.

Moisturise. Advise your nieces to put a simple, unperfumed moisturizer on any dry spots on their skin that they find, but not to worry about moisturizing daily until they get quite a bit older. You can buy them a little moisturizing lip balm, which they can put on every day. This will be all that they need to stay fresh-faced and gorgeous. Not that you're biased . . .

'The taste was that of the little crumb of madeleine which on Sunday mornings at Combray, when I used to say good-day to her in her bedroom, my aunt Léonie used to give me, dipping it first in her own cup of tea or tisane.'

FROM *IN SEARCH OF LOST TIME* BY
MARCEL PROUST (1871–1922)

FAMOUS AUNTS

Spare a thought for celebrity aunt Denise Richards. The American actress and former Bond girl had to navigate herself through the tricky situation of her thirteen-year-old nephew finding an issue of *Playboy* – that she featured in. Denise explained that her job involved taking lots of sexy acting parts and that she did the *Playboy* shoot five months after having her own baby, to prove that mums could be sexy too. Though she was embarrassed to have to tackle this subject, she turned the tables by telling her nephew: 'You should be glad – I bet I'm the only aunt in school that has done *Playboy*.'

HAIR TODAY . . .

Another fun way to get girly but stay silly is to try lots of different hairstyles with your niece. Gather together brushes, combs, clips, slides, rollers and hair ties and get experimenting! If you're not the girly sort yourself and find just passing a brush through your hair a bit of an effort, here are some classic, basic styles to try your hand at. Why not set up a little at-home hair salon with a kitchen chair placed in front of a full-length mirror, lots of hair magazines to look through for inspiration and a long natter about where you're going on your holidays.

How to create a French plait

A tidy, intricate-looking style that will look lovely and keep hair neat and out of the way on a busy day. Works best for shoulder-length hair or longer.

1. Use both hands to scoop up the top half of your niece's hair into a ponytail. Imagine a line drawn between the top of her ears; this line is the division between the top half and the bottom half.

2. Use your fingers to divide this ponytail into three equal sections, while still keeping a hold of the hair and not letting it drop.

3. Starting at the top of the head, take the outer section on the left-hand side and pass it over the middle section.

4. Take the outer section on the right-hand side and pass it over the middle section.

Continue plaiting the sections in this way and as you move down the head pick up sections of hair from each side of the bottom half of the head. Add these in gradually to the sections as you plait them so all the hair is seamlessly incorporated.

Keep plaiting until you reach the nape of the neck. Fasten the plait with a hair tie.

How to create a French twist

A sleek, sophisticated look for shoulder-length hair or longer.

1. Thoroughly brush the hair until it is entirely free of tangles and knots. You want the hair to look as smooth as possible at this point.

2. Loosely gather the hair into a ponytail, but don't pull it too tight. You want the hair to have a little bit of loose shape around the face. If it's too tight, the twisting part will be a bit uncomfortable for your hair model.

3. Hold the ponytail in both hands with the ends of the hair pointing up at the ceiling. Start to twist from the base of the ponytail in an anticlockwise direction. This will create a 'roll' of hair lying vertically against the head.

4. Fully twist it around twice.

5. Tuck the ends of the hair, now lying towards the top of the head, behind the roll on the right-hand side. You'll now have a seamless and smooth twist effect.

6. Secure the hair with a large hair comb or with a few hair-pins. If you are using pins, try to conceal them behind the hair as you slide them in, so they aren't too obvious.

Voilà!

How to create easy waves

A fun and slightly messy look without lots of heated rollers and hot tongs.

1. Gently shampoo and rinse your niece's hair, then apply conditioner and leave on for 5 minutes for a real deep-conditioning treatment. While you're waiting, use the tips of your fingers to massage your niece's scalp for the authentic professional salon experience.

2. Rinse out the conditioner and towel-dry the hair. Then comb through to get rid of any tangles.

3. Starting near the face, gather together a small handful of hair. Divide this section into three parts and begin to plait (as you did in the French plait section on page 139).

4. When you get to the end of this small plait, fix it with a hair tie.

5. Now gather a small handful of hair next to this first plait and repeat the plaiting process.

6. Continue to make these small plaits all the way round the head until all the hair is plaited.

7. Put on a fun film or read a good book together for 20 minutes while the hair dries.

8.   When the hair is dry, undo the hair ties and gently shake
      the hair loose from the plaits. You'll be left with lovely
      crinkly, wavy hair.

9.   For bigger waves, make thicker plaits and for tighter,
      crimped waves try and keep the plaits as small as you can.

Laying Down the Law

Every aunt wants to be a favourite aunt – it's only natural when you love your nieces and nephews so much – but sometimes even favourite aunts have to get tough. If you're an aunt who only ever says 'yes' you'll end up with spoilt little monsters on your hands, instead of the little angels you know today. Knowing when to say 'no' and, more importantly, how to say it best is an essential skill. A little discipline can go a long way.

Have a chat with your siblings about the rules they have for behaviour and the consequences for breaking them. The golden rule is to establish your boundaries and stick to them. Children respond very well to stability and routine; once it's clear what sorts of behaviour you won't allow, make sure you don't let them get away with the same things on another day because you're feeling worn out or under the weather. Too much punishment can be as damaging as too little, and you should bear in mind that younger children are still learning to control their behaviour and so need a more patient and forgiving approach.

Children won't stop loving you just because you're handing out the punishments – they still love their parents, after all, who have to be far meaner and stricter than aunties sometimes. If you're an aunt who hasn't had her own children yet and so feels a bit in the dark about laying down the law, here are some guidelines.

TODDLERS

Toddlers are just getting to grips with the world and their place in it. Impulsive behaviour is to be expected at this age, but not necessarily overlooked. It's entirely normal for a toddler to throw a tantrum because they can't have a biscuit when they want one, but that doesn't mean you have to pander to that tantrum. If a child is crying and wailing because they can't have what they want, explain to them in a firm voice that Auntie has said no and that's the final decision. The crying will probably persist, but you'll have to grit your teeth and bear it after your first reaction because to give the toddler more attention will re-inforce the idea that making a lot of noise and fuss will get them what they want. Instead, go for distraction. Quickly changing the subject is the best way to leave tears behind. Point out of a window and ask the child if they just saw that big parrot flying by, or if they can see the helicopter that just whizzed past. Of course, there was no such thing, but this little white lie avoids lots of later upset for you both.

If the problem is that a toddler won't share toys or is too rough with other children when playing, then calmly take their hand and lead them away from the play area. In a quiet, level voice, explain that only children who behave nicely and who

share their toys can play here and they will have to stand on their own while they calm down and prepare to be on their best behaviour. Being away from the fun and games will begin to show the child that unpleasant behaviour just results in missing out on the fun and being far from friends and family. When they have calmed down and are looking longingly at the play going on without them, lead them back again with a smile and a reassuring expression. They've had their time out for what they did so now you're all on an even keel again and the fun can continue. If the toddler in question has a lot of energy and is especially stroppy during their tantrum you may have to wait longer for them to become calm. If they are rolling on the floor, kicking and lashing out, just make sure there's nothing nearby that they could hurt themselves on, but otherwise leave them to work out their stroppiness. Earplugs might be necessary . . .

SPECIAL AUNT STORIES

Some aunts need a little more disciplining themselves. A very naughty aunt in Canberra, Australia was accused of taking her two little nieces to a casino to 'keep her company' while she gambled. To make matters even worse, she was alleged to have been stealing their inheritance to gamble with. The aunt pleaded not guilty to theft and her case has yet to go to trial, but it doesn't sound like the right sort of auntie behaviour, in any case!

It may be easy to shout 'Bad girl!' or 'Bad boy!' after a toddler has shoved a playmate, but this is only likely to cause more tears and frustration. Repeat to yourself: *children can't be bad, only behaviour can be bad*. This will remind you that any discipline you dish out should show the child what they did that was wrong and how to avoid doing it again. Discipline should not make the child feel bad about themselves; this will only lead to them feeling upset and angry in future, and definitely won't mean an end to bad behaviour.

Lots of patience is required for keeping toddlers in order, but do remember that life can seem very frustrating when you are a tiny tot who can't yet articulate fully or reach the things you're after. Put yourself in their small shoes and you'll realize there's quite a bit to get cross about at that age. Take deep breaths and keep calm at all times.

SMALL CHILDREN, AGED FIVE TO ELEVEN

Slightly older children will have a better understanding of what's expected of them and are mature enough to be able to behave in that way without being explicitly told. You may find nieces and nephews occasionally acting up at this age when away from their parents. It's natural for children to test boundaries and see what they can get away with – I'm sure you can remember trying to pull a trick or two when you were younger! Disciplining children at this age involves reasoning with them and giving them the space to make their own decisions.

If a child has behaved badly, for instance watching TV in their room after lights out, give them a clear warning in a

strong, definite voice that this is unacceptable and the next time it happens there will be consequences. If they break this rule again, stay calm and ask them what *they* think their punishment should be. Strangely, children tend to pick quite mean and fitting punishments when they're given the choice! If you'd rather choose the punishment yourself then removing privileges or treats is usually a fair way of getting the point across. Once they've had the punishment, don't mention the misdemeanour again. Bringing up their offence again won't help them feel positive and strive for good behaviour in the future.

Shouting at a child for acting naughtily is a short-term and pretty ineffectual tactic. An angry child being shouted at will just shout back – it will soon become a volume competition. Take deep breaths to stay calm and think things through before you say them.

If a child has been teasing or hurting a sibling or friend, take a moment to explain to them just why you're so disappointed in their behaviour. Ask them how they'd feel and if they'd want someone to do the same to them. Bringing out their empathetic side will not only help them see the other side of things, but will be a useful skill as they socialize in the future.

TEENAGERS, AGED TWELVE TO EIGHTEEN

Every aunt can cast her mind back to her teenage years and recount some moments of terrible teenage angst when 'life wasn't fair!' Those days may be far behind you and you've now had the benefit of years of life experience to help you stay calm, but your teenage nieces and nephews are only just beginning to enter the adult world. Because of this, they need lots of your

wisdom and patience. All sorts of things can trigger less than perfect behaviour in teenagers: the desire to impress peers and look cool; going through puberty; suddenly being old enough to stay out late; the stress of exams and first jobs. Quite a headache, you'll agree. So bear these things in mind and be sympathetic to the tumultuous times these young adults are going through.

Teenagers can in fact revert to toddler behaviour when things don't go their way: slamming doors, screaming and shouting. It may be tempting to laugh a little at this, but do keep any giggling to yourself. These emotions are very serious to the teens, here and now – even though they will most likely laugh with you about it in five years' time. Treat them like adults at all times, even if they are regressing by ten or so years. Show them that having the freedoms and powers of adulthood brings a new level of responsibility. Explain logically why you have to discipline them and don't react to any overly emotional behaviour with the same.

If a teen has broken a curfew or taken something they shouldn't, sit down and talk to them about how the way they've behaved has temporarily affected the trust between you. Therefore, you'll have to take back some privileges for a while until you're confident the trust has been won back. This could be bringing forward a curfew, cutting back pocket money or denying Internet access at home for a few days. Explain that this is as much about their safety as it is about breaking rules; you need to be able to trust them to act sensibly and confidently when they're out on their own. Try to use examples of when you might have pushed boundaries as a teen and how, though at the time it felt tough, you realized you needed to take a fresh look at how you were behaving and how it affected everyone

around you. A stroppy teen can be a disruptive thing for the whole family so make sure you listen out for any underlying problems that may be setting off the rule-breaking. See the Agony Aunt section (page 73) for more tips on giving advice.

FAMOUS AUNTS

Aunts should never fear that laying down the law will make them unpopular with nephews and nieces. John Lennon was raised by his Aunt 'Mimi' in Liverpool and she was known to be a firm believer in rules and keeping everything on the straight and narrow. Despite being strict, Mimi had a great sense of humour and was always kind and caring. She and John remained close throughout their lives and his childhood experiences with her cropped up in a number of the Beatles' songs, most noticeably 'Strawberry Fields', which was inspired by a garden party they went to together. The only blot on Aunt Mimi's auntie reputation was that she repeatedly told John that music was all well and good, but that he'd never make a living out of it! Mendips, the house Aunt Mimi lived in with John, is now a National Trust heritage house.

Out on the Town

If your nieces and nephews have done very well in a school report, play or sports event, take your chance to give them a little treat with a night out on the town. There are lots of trips you can organize that will make them feel they're doing something special and grown up. You don't have to do too much damage to your purse, either. Simple activities can be dressed up with a touch more glamour and excitement when you put on your best clothes, all bundle into the car or take a train trip and venture out for a night on the town . . .

FINE DINING

You'll probably have a good idea of what your nieces and nephews will eat or how open-minded they are to trying new food. If you're not so sure, a good bet is always an Italian restaurant. There can't be many kids who'll turn down some pasta or a pizza. You're sure to find something for even the fussiest of eaters and you can always ask the restaurant staff to make a very basic tomato sauce for the picky among you. The other benefit is that there'll be delicious Italian foods for aunts. And, of course, the Italians do make some rather marvellous ice cream.

ART AFTER DARK

Many art galleries in big cities will have late opening hours – give them a ring or look up their website to find out when. This means you can make what might otherwise be seen as an educational trip something more exciting and special. Encourage the kids to put on their best clothes for the event and discuss what you think of each piece of art. Finish the night with a hot chocolate and cake in a chic cafe.

TAKE IN THE SILVER SCREEN

Children's films now seem to have all the best special effects, CGI graphics and amazing action so why not do yourself a favour and use the kids as an excuse to see the latest children's film at the cinema? Sitting in a plush seat as the lights come down and the magic begins on the silver screen always holds a certain thrill and your nieces and nephews will love to share this with you. If you're worried about forking out for several loads of popcorn and fizzy drinks, you can always take in a few bottles of water and some bags of sweets to save on concession prices.

STRIKE!

Though you might not find the shoes very flattering, you'll have to admit that bowling is good, old-fashioned fun through and through. If you have very little nieces and nephews you might want to ask the staff at the bowling alley to put up the barriers at the side of the lane to block off the gutters. This will give the novice bowlers a chance of knocking down a few pins and feeling like they've had a smashing day. Don't worry too much about keeping score as the real entertainment will come from trying the game together – and laughing at the awful shoes . . .

You Can't Spoil a Good Thing

Sometimes the urge to let a niece or nephew know just how fantastic they are will overrule your more sensible side and you'll wrack your brains for a treat. But treats don't have to be elaborate or expensive to hit the spot and really make a child feel special. Think back to your own childhood: it wasn't necessarily the flashiest toys or the most exotic holidays that felt like the most fun or created the strongest memories. Sometimes just the fact that a loved one has put lots of time, care and attention into a treat will give it that magic sparkle. Why not try one or a few of the following to indulge your spoily side as an aunt:

● If you're babysitting or having a visit from your wonderful nephew or niece soon, why not get all the ingredients in for their favourite meal? Cook them a hearty and healthy dinner that really tickles their taste buds and it can become a family tradition to always eat this meal together. As they get older they can help you prepare it, so it'll be a treat as well as some good kitchen experience.

● Scrapbooking is a popular craft that provides a beautiful way of displaying photos, postcards and memorabilia. In a plain scrapbook, stick in some baby photos of your niece or nephew and write in details of what you remember about the day they were born – how you felt, what they looked like, even what the weather was like. Then stick in any ticket stubs or receipts from things you've done together and note down the activities and locations. Leave lots of pages blank for you to both fill together with all of your adventures to come. It's a great way to keep memories fresh and cement your relationship.

- Ice cream is a treat that always goes down well. Visit an ice cream parlour with your nieces and nephews and let them choose a big sundae with their favourite flavours of ice cream, with sprinkles, nuts, sweets and sauces on top if they like. Forget about healthy eating for once while you all tuck in.

- If your niece or nephew has a favourite sports team they support – either local or international – try and get tickets to an upcoming match for you to watch together. Deck yourselves out in the team colours. You could even use face paints to spell out the team name on your cheeks if you're brave. Declare yourself a lifelong fan of the team and try to make time to see them play together whenever you can.

And don't forget that very good aunties deserve a few treats along the way too . . .

ACKNOWLEDGEMENTS

I'd like to thank Kerry for her marvellous help, instruction and wisdom (as ever), and everyone at Michael O'Mara for their hard work and support. Thanks also to Mary for sharing her infinite wisdom on how to keep children busy and sanity intact. Most of all, thanks to my nephew Jack for letting me trial my ideas and techniques on him.